THE AUTHOR: Sheila Bird is a former schoolteacher who has written several books of West Country interest. She is now a full-time writer and journalist and regularly contributes to a variety of local and national newspapers and magazines.

The Book of Somerset Villages

Sheila Bird

Line drawings by Louise Dobbs

DOVECOTE PRESS

To my brother, Eric

First published in 1986 by the Dovecote Press Ltd
Stanbridge, Wimborne, Dorset

ISBN 0 946159 41 6

Photoset by Word Perfect 99 Ltd, Bournemouth, Dorset
Printed and bound by Biddles Ltd, Guildford and King's Lynn

Illustrations

Introduction

Somerset is a county of great beauty and contrasts and is steeped in colourful folklore and history. Despite modern 'progress', it is still possible to delight in the lesser highways and byways and come across unspoilt villages and friendly country folk.

Nature has been kind to the county, with its pleasing, most English of landscapes in all their charming diversity. Consider the contrasts between the dramatic hill country of the Mendips, Exmoor, the Brendons, the Quantocks and the Blackdowns, each with an identity of its own; coastal Somerset ranging from the spectacular cliffs around Porlock to the extensive flats where the tide retreats for miles, to the gentler charms of the Vale of Taunton or the rolling green landscape of the borders with Wiltshire and Dorset and the unique character of the Central Lowlands, dissected by the Polden ridge. Many of the villages are architectural gems, while the fine churches of Somerset remain a tribute to the skill and dedication of craftsmen who went before us. Our ancestors also played a part in the evolution of the landscape as we know it today; had it not been for on-going drainage and reclamation schemes much of central Somerset would still be under water.

The pleasing name 'Somerset', with its mellow ring, is thought to have derived from 'Seo-Mere-Saetan', meaning 'Dwellers by the Sea Lakes', while 'Avalon', originally denoting the Isle of Arthurian legend around Glastonbury was thought to indicate 'the land of apples', probably of sacred significance. More recently part of the county has been lost to the new district of Avon. Situations change; some places have emerged into contemporary focus for various reasons; others, once important have declined in status. In compiling this book I have included some hamlets and small towns with a village ethos.

Traces of very early man have been discovered in the county, while successive generations have implanted evidence of their civilisations on the landscape for those who follow on to interpret as they will. The remains of fine Roman villas and the legacy of the old Roman thoroughfares remain with us. Legend and history are inexorably intertwined. Before the fall of Rome Somerset had become a cradle of Christianity in Britain. There is a deep rooted legend that Joseph of Arimathea implanted his staff in the Glastonbury soil, establishing the thorn of Glastonbury, reputed to bloom at Christmas, as well as starting the first English church, and that Jesus accompanied him on his travels and visited the village of Priddy.

After the departure of the Romans, repeated resistance to the Saxons gave rise to the legends of King Arthur, and after his death the Saxons took possession of Somerset. In the 9th century when the county suffered from the Viking threat, King Alfred took refuge on the Isle of Athelney before driving home a decisive victory. Evidence of Saxon and Norman times is still found in the county's churches. The Normans created the hunting forests of Selwood, Mendip, Neroche, Exmoor and North Petherton. In medieval times the mining potential was being exploited and traditional trades flourished around the little towns and villages. The Civil War actually erupted in Somerset and in 1685 it was destined to be the site of Monmouth's defeat.

There are many literary links with the landscape, and it is fascinating to discover the large and varied number of Somerset folk who went on to make their mark in the world in one way or another. In creating this book about the villages of Somerset, emphasis has been placed on topography, history, folklore and anecdotes, and it incorporates a variety of themes including the evolution of canals and railways and the lives and customs of the people. I have endeavoured to capture the unique, mellow spirit of the villages and the warm and friendly folk who live in them. We hope that their future will be guided by those who care about the environment and the quality of life in Somerset.

My thanks go to my brother, Dr Eric Bird for his geomorphological help, to museums, local councils, Tourist Information Centres, staff of The West Somerset Railway, David Hayball, librarians in Somerset, Dorset and Devon, booksellers and the many folk around the villages who have made the researching of this book so enjoyable and memorable.

Aisholt

The attractive, unspoilt village of Aisholt lying midway between Taunton and the coast, almost hidden at the foot of a deep hollow on the eastern side of the Quantocks, has a little 15th century church clinging to the steep hillside, with a churchyard rising to the level of its belfry. The top of this churchyard provides a vantage point where it is possible to look over the trees to Will's Neck, which at 1261 feet above sea level is the highest point of the beautiful rolling Quantock Hills and from which spectacular views of the Severn estuary, Mendips, Exmoor and the lowlands of Somerset can be enjoyed.

This part of Somerset has provided inspiration for poets, and Aisholt was the one time home of Sir Henry Newbolt (1862-1938), writer of the patriotic and stirring *'Drake's Drum'*. Samuel Taylor Coleridge, who had a desire to settle here, but feared it might prove rather too lonely for his wife, moved to nearby Nether Stowey instead. The poet Wordsworth, who was then living south of Crewkerne moved to Alfoxton House with his sister Dorothy to be nearer his new-found friend.

A modern addition to the landscape is the Hawkridge Reservoir about a mile to the north of the village.

Aller

The dramatic slopes of the wooded High Ham range of hills rise steeply above the ancient little village of Aller, on the fringe of Somerset's central levels about three miles out of Langport on the Bridgwater road. From its position on the lower slopes there are commanding views across Aller Moor, North Moor, to the 'Sowy' villages and Burrow Mump.

This has been the scene of strife and reconciliation, for it was here, at the church of the royal estate, that the remarkable Saxon king Alfred had the vanquished Danish leader Guthrum and a number of his followers baptised after the battle of Edington. The Civil War actually erupted in Somerset, and during bloody skirmishes at Langport and Aller Moor in 1645 Fairfax defeated the Royalist leader Goring.

Ralph Cudworth, who ranks high among the Worthies of Somerset, was born at Aller in 1617, where his father was rector. At the age of 22 he obtained his Master of Arts degree at Emanuel College, Cambridge and was elected Fellow of his college. Following a brilliant academic career, he wrote religious and philosophical books, the greatest of which was the impressively entitled work *The True Intellectual System Of The Universe.*

Allerford, *see* Bossington

Ansford

Close to the expanding town of Castle Cary, the small and compact village of Ansford still maintains a character of its own with some interesting houses around its rectory and church.

Ansford has literary associations, for the Somerset diarist James Woodforde was born at the rectory at the corner of Tucker's Lane in 1740. He served as curate to his father and took up residence at Lower Ansford Manor which was burnt down in 1892, referring to the place in his diary as the 'Lower House'. He later became curate of Babcary.

In his diary Parson Woodforde, who believed in keeping a good table and catalogued the alcoholic and culinary delights enjoyed at the vicarage, gives us a rare insight into everyday life in a Somerset village. Anecdotes covering social events, church affairs, card games and pastimes not only bring the past to life, but enable us to share his concern about the weaknesses and foibles of his family and friends, illustrating as always that fashions and social climates may change, but basically human nature remains very much the same. His parents and his niece, Nancy, who kept house for him for twenty four years at Weston Longville are buried in the family vault here.

Ash

The small village of Ash, on secondary roads between Martock and Yeovil, possesses the unusual and interesting feature of a simple little tower which was added to the church as a war memorial. The church was constructed from 1840 to 1887.

There are some 17th century houses along Burrough Street, with examples of 18th and 19th century houses along the main road and there are modern housing developments and in-filling.

Although the name of the village has a sylvan ring to it, 'Ash' is a derivation of the earlier 'Esse' found in ancient documents.

Ashcott

The delightful, gentle low hills which form a ridge and dissect the lowlands of Somerset are known as the Poldens, but the lands on each side of this dividing range are very different in character. To the south and west, it is a green and fertile landscape, but immediately to the north there are rough, dark areas of heathland where peat is excavated.

Peatland is locally known as 'turbary', and Ashcott is one of the main centres for the peat trade. Peat from these moors was originally used for fuel, and during the last war was sold to supplement fuel supplies in local towns. The age old peat cutting industry retains its customs and traditional language. The dark and dripping spadeloads of peat are referred to as 'mumps' and these are split and the chocolate coloured slabs are arranged in cruciform pattern to obtain maximum air circulation for drying; a process which is known as 'hiling.' After a few weeks the hiles are stacked in characteristic beehive mounds known as 'ruckles' or 'tunnigers', which also encourage circulation of air to complete the drying out process. The areas of cut peat tend to fill with water as they deepen and the ruckles are often positioned in symmetrical lines alongside these 'canals'. The peatlands, with their traditional patterns of ruckles, stacked alongside water-filled ditches, can be viewed to advantage from Ashcott and the Poldens.

Today, the peat which is delivered around the West Country or sold in garden centres in black, plastic sacks is in demand as cattle feed, poultry litter, fertiliser and compost as well as fuel. The special nature of the peaty soil has preserved a system of ancient trackways, some of them dating an incredible three thousand years before the birth of Christ.

In December 1800 the Piper's Inn was described by turnpike travellers as 'clean and comfortable;' an unsolicited testimonial which the present day hotel must be pleased to perpetuate for today's motorised visitors.

Ash Priors

The village, which lies to the north-west of Taunton and whose name has a monastic ring, was once a possession of the Priory of Taunton. A two storey porch is all that remains of the priory here. The church of Holy Trinity, which has a west tower with diagonal buttresses and battlements, was much restored in 1874. Ash Priors Common, which resembles a village green, and lies to the south east of the village is one of the few areas to have escaped enclosure.

Streams from the foothills of the Quantocks dissect this pleasing countryside, and to the south of Ash Priors, over King's Moor and Halse Water lies the charming village of Halse where there was a branch house of the Knights Hospitallers and a nunnery. Stoford, between the two villages, has an old barn associated with legends of the Knights Hospitallers.

Ashwick, *see* Oakhill

Athelney

Lying in the heart of one of Somerset's most romantic areas of legend and mystery, Athelney, near the junction of the rivers Tone and Parrett in the marshlands to the north-east of Taunton, has strong links with Alfred the Great. Alfred, the youngest of the four sons of Ethelwulf, King of Wessex, was born in 849 and became king following the death of his brothers. History has proved him to be a remarkable man of many talents, including fine qualities of leadership. So ferocious was the Viking onslaught of that period that a new prayer was introduced into the church service, beginning: 'Good Lord, deliver us from the fury of the Danes.' In 878 Alfred took

Athelney, King Alfred's Monument

refuge on the Isle of Athelney, a section of rising land then completely surrounded by water. Survival during that winter must have been difficult, but he spent the time working out a plan of campaign. In a situation like this it is hardly surprising that colourful legends built up around events and there is a story about Alfred entering the Danish camp dressed as a minstrel, and of course the classic one that every schoolchild knows about his being responsible for the burning of the cakes in the peasant woman's hut. A translation of *Asser's Life of Alfred* runs thus: 'Alfred, King of the West Saxons, with a few of his nobles, and certain soldiers and vassals, used to lead an unquiet life among the woodlands of the county of Somerset in great tribulation. It chanced that, on a certain day, the wife of the cowherd in whose hut the King had lived for a time, was preparing some loaves to bake, and Alfred, sitting at the hearth, made ready his bows and arrows and other warlike instruments. The unlucky woman, espying the cakes burning at the fire, ran up to remove them, and, rebuking the King, exclaimed:

"Ca'sn thee mind the ke-aks, man,
An' doosen zee 'em burn?
I'm boun thee's eat 'em vast enough,
As zoon as 'tis the turn."

The blundering woman little thought that it was King Alfred, who had fought so many battles against the Pagans, and gained so many victories over them.' Fact or fiction, a monument was erected in 1801 on the supposed spot of the cake burning incident.

Having subsequently defeated the Danes, Alfred founded an abbey at Athelney as a thanksgiving for his victory. In medieval times the monks of the abbey carried out land reclamation work with a system of draining this marshy area.

All around Athelney acres and acres of withies stretch in an array of graceful silver and green. Withies are willows which have been cut back to allow a growth of tender shoots suitable for wickerwork, a traditional occupation in these parts since the 13th century and possibly earlier. But it was not until the Victorian trend for wickerwork furniture that they were cultivated to such an extent.

Babcary

During the Norman period of architecture, which extended from 1066 until 1189, a large number of castles, cathedrals and churches were built, with Somerset having a large percentage of them. Few of the austere, solidly constructed Norman churches, with their characteristic, rounded arches have survived in East Somerset due to the old custom of demolishing old churches and erecting new ones on the same site. Babcary church is one of the few good examples of remaining Norman churches to be found in the area.

The village has close links with Somerset's noteworthy diarist and curate James Woodforde, son of the rector of Ansford, who rode over from that village to take up his new appointment in 1764 and recorded for posterity that he dined on 'a sheep's heart which I carried in my pocket.' Bell ringing was a well rewarded occupation at the time, for on the occasion of ringing in their new curate the campanologists received half a crown from him and a pail of cider from the churchwarden for their labours. In his diary, which is rated highly, and not so far behind that of Samuel Pepys, he recorded everyday happenings around the village giving an insight into customs and attitudes at the time, with endearing details about pastimes and characters. He was a lovable man rather than a saintly one, and seemed pre-occupied with the pleasures of eating and drinking. Nothing seemed to take the edge off his appetite; one entry stated: 'Found the old gentleman almost at his last gasp. Totally senseless with rattlings in his throat. Dinner today boiled beef and rabbit roasted.'

Babcary, situated close to the Fosse Way to the north of Yeovil, is also within a mile of an isolated barrow, topped with an obelisk — and intriguingly named Wimble Toot. Today the River Cary sparkles its way through the village with its stone houses, farms and thatched inn, meanders on through a landscape rich in pre-history, before taking its straightened course through King's Sedge Moor and joining the Parrett to emerge in Bridgwater Bay.

Baltonsborough

This village, to the south east of Glastonbury is the birthplace of St Dunstan, a talented musician, illuminator, designer and metal worker destined to become a great monastic leader who made his mark on the nation. He is thought to have devised the monarch's consecration ceremony on which subsequent coronations were based.

Dunstan was born of royal stock in 909, the year in which his kinsman Athelm was consecrated the first bishop of the Somerset people. Around 925 he was introduced to the royal household under Athelstan, and was later appointed abbot of the community at Glastonbury. This provided a valued link between Glastonbury and the Saxon kings, resulting in increased wealth and importance. Dunstan set about re-establishing the Benedictine rule of monasticism, which was to become the model on which religious life in England became based, and having been banished by Eadwig and exiled in Ghent, he was able to gain experience of the Continental monastic revival, which stood him in good stead. On being recalled to England by Eadwig's brother, Edgar, King of Mercia, he was appointed Bishop of Worcester, then of London and finally became Archbishop of Canterbury.

Not surprisingly, colourful legends surround St Dunstan, the greatest of the Saxon saints, who was said to be capable of not only keeping the Devil in his place, but of sometimes obtaining his co-operation. As a great brewer of ale, he was particularly keen to achieve the very finest vintage, and to ensure success made special arrangements with Old Nick to send frost annually on St Dunstan's Day (19th May) to nip his rival cider apple growers' apple blossom in the bud. Not only this, but harnessing a Midas-like touch, he could turn mercury into gold. Dr Dee, alchemist of Elizabeth I's time claimed to have stolen from St Dunstan's grave scrolls of parchment on which the alchemic secret was revealed — but history does not record how he put the discovery to use. It was said that the Devil was always making playful attempts to topple St Dunstan from the straight-and-narrow, and favoured the guise of a seductive maiden or a starving beggar. However, Dunstan did not stand for such nonsense. Using the tools of his craft, he brandished his red hot tongs and tweaked the Devil's nose, causing him to howl and flee in terror.

The village, situated close to the River Brue on the perimeter of the moors, has its 15th century church appropriately named after this special saint. The attractive 17th century gatehouse has mullioned windows. Many of the stone houses around the village incorporate structures and stone from earlier buildings, some of which is thought to have come from Glastonbury.

Barrington

Somerset's riches have always lain in the soil, and the potential of the green and fertile land around Crewkerne, Ilchester and Yeovil was recognised from earliest times. At Barrington, 3 miles to the north east of Ilminster, the ancient field strips, cultivated by tenants of the manor and divided by banks rather than hedges, are still visible and give us an insight into the feudal way of life.

The buildings in this very attractive village are largely concentrated on a single street. The Priory, Knapp House and Vinces are fine examples of medieval structures, while Easons is of 17th century origin. There are some pretty cottages, and a number of them are thatched. To the north of the village where the south Somerset meadows are on a level with the moors, is the end of the former Westport canal (*see* Westport). In contrast, the scarp of Winsmoor hill rises sharply to a plateau at the other end.

There was a local timber trade dealing mostly with oak, ash, elm and maple from Neroche, while apples and plums were grown in orchards and hedgerows. It was quite an economic blow to the place when the Westport canal closed. People moved away in search of work and many local folk emigrated to America and Canada or sought employment in South Wales.

At the eastern side of the village is Barrington Court, with its stylish approach, beautiful gardens and magnificent Ham stone mansion with finials and chimney stacks, and now in the care of the

National Trust. It has late Gothic windows and a red brick stable block dating from 1670. It was restored earlier this century. King John visited Barrington in 1207 and the place was caught up in political events during the 17th century when the Strode family lived there and entertained the Duke of Monmouth. Ten local men were accused of complicity in the aftermath of the Monmouth Rebellion.

Batcombe

Tucked away among the hills in peaceful, little known countryside north of Bruton lies the tiny village of Batcombe, with its splendid church tower rising 87 feet from the combe in spectacular style. This sturdy unpinnacled tower dates from around 1540 and is one of the most noble and ornate in the county. The south porch, blending Gothic and Classical styles, was built by James Bisse in 1629.

The manor passed to the Bisse family after the Dissolution of Glastonbury Abbey, and there are family monuments around the church. A 16th century rector, Philip Bisse, Archdeacon of Taunton, presented Wadham College, Oxford with two thousand books, had his portrait hung in the library, and became named as co-founder of the college.

Today the steep, narrow lanes are a particular delight in springtime with the wayside flowers, while the lovely hill country is appreciated by local walkers and picnickers.

Battleborough, ***see*** **Brent Knoll**

Bawdrip

Bawdrip is situated on the southern side of the Poldens overlooking Sedgemoor, and once had a station on the old Somerset and Dorset railway.

Its interesting, mainly 13th century church of St Michael, constructed of Ham Hill stone and Blue Lias has a square high tower. The church contains a defaced effigy of a knight in 14th century plate armour, an oak panel with Tudor carvings and an inscription to the ill-fated heiress Eleanor Lovell 'who died June 14th 1681, taken away by a sudden and untimely fate at the very time of the marriage celebrations.' (The tablet, erected by her husband on the north side of the sanctuary was moved during restorations in 1866) The 'Mistletoe Bough' legend would have us believe that the excited young bride, who was a bit of a tease, hid in a chest carved with mistletoe boughs on her wedding day, to keep folk guessing. Unfortunately she was imprisoned in there by a spring lock and was suffocated on her wedding day.

Beckington

Close to the Wiltshire border and at the junction of the modern day A36 and A361 trunk routes, the stone-built village of Beckington is rich in historical and architectural interest. The church has a rare and fine example of a Norman tower. Other notable buildings include the abbey, built by Augustinian canons in 1502, a 17th century rectory, a large 16th century house known as Beckington Castle, the Old Manse House with gables and mullioned windows and Seymour's Court, a farmhouse, once the home of Sir Thomas Seymour, who married Catherine Parr, the widow of Henry VIII.

It is the birthplace of the 14th century Bishop Beckington, who built many churches and enhanced the beauty of Wells, and Alfred William Parsons R.A., one time President of the Royal Society of Painters in Water Colours, who was born in 1847. The earliest Somerset born poet, Samuel Daniel (1562-1619), a friend of Sir Philip Sidney and tutor to Lady Anne Clifford, returned to his native county, taking up residence at nearby Rudge (then known as Ridge), and was buried in St George's Church.

The church of St Mary the Virgin at nearby Berkley was described by Nikolaus Pevsner, the authority on historical architecture as 'small, but the best Georgian church in any Somerset village.' Praise indeed. The manor house contains 17th and 18th century work.

Close to the county border, Standerwick Court, with mullioned windows and an exceptionally fine early 18th century staircase, commands fine views of the Wiltshire Downs.

Berrow

The open expanse of the Bridgwater Bay foreshore around Berrow and Brean, with sandbanks and waterchannels attracting sea birds, and wide skyscapes reflected in the pools and shallow channels, is recognised for the quality of its light and magical sunsets. After the last war caravans, chalets and then bungalows took a hold here.

The rise and fall of the tide in the Bristol Channel, with a range of about 35 feet is among the largest in the world and a breach in the seawall could allow floodwater to penetrate deep into Somerset. From earliest times seawalls were constructed and landowners were compelled by law to maintain them. On 20th January 1607, the seawall near Burnham gave way under 'huge and mighty hilles of water, tombling one over another, in such sort, as if the greatest mountaines in the world had overwhelmed the lowe valeyes or marshy grounds. Sometimes it so dazzled the eyes of spectators that they imagined it had been some fogge or miste, coming with great swiftness towards them.' Local folk frantically took refuge, farmers tried to save what stock they could, while the wildlife made for higher ground. A milkmaid of Berrow 'round about beset' by water, found herself marooned on a bank in the company of rats, voles, mice and other creatures who had made a similar bid for survival. The swiftly moving floodwaters which engulfed villages and drowned people covered an area twenty miles inland and five miles across.

In former times Glastonbury Abbey claimed rights of 'wreck and sea' from Berrow to Brean Down. Today the 13th century church among the dunes, built of limestone faced with Doulting stone, bears evidence of its situation close to the elements, having been eroded by sea, sun and storm.

Bickenhall, *see* Staple Fitzpaine

Bicknoller

The delightful Quantock hills, so beloved by ramblers, were a particular joy to the poets Coleridge and Wordsworth who used to walk over to Bicknoller from Nether Stowey on the eastern side of the range. Bicknoller lies between the A358 and the steep western slopes of the escarpment, and is close to the course of the West Somerset Railway. From the summit there are superb views over the Bristol Channel and the Vale of Taunton Deane, towards the Brendons, across the Blackdowns and Exmoor. There is much evidence of prehistoric occupation hereabouts, with Trendle Ring Settlement, Thorncombe Barrow, forts, cairns and tumuli. For today's walker there is a network of paths and tracks, which give the opportunity to visit neighbouring villages and keep up one's strength with a pie and a pint, and to enjoy a friendly yarn.

The partly Norman church is rich in carving and tracery, and has a fine rood screen and intricately carved bench ends. The old cross and the village stocks are further reminders of the past in this lovely village.

Binegar, *see* **Oakhill**

Bishop's Hull

Bishop's Hull and its Elizabethan manor house have now been swallowed up by Taunton, and it is a far cry from the days of 1633 when local antiquarian Thomas Gerard recorded that '. . . besides the River which is heare fayre and very clear, you have the prospect of many fair orchards, gardens, and cherry gardens, of which there are a great number here about, and there cherries ripe welneere as soon as at London, for (there) is rich redd earth which produceth all fruits not only in great plentye but very early, insomuch that they have peas and other such fruites as soon as London; from this walke also you may see many and those most flourishing meadowes, lying by ye Riverside.'

William Crotch, the child protegé was buried here. Born in Norwich in 1775, he was able to pick out tunes on his father's organ at the age of two, and gave concerts in London as a small child sitting on his mother's lap. He went to Oxford University and gained a degree as Bachelor of Music and went from triumph to triumph. He became the first Principal of the Royal College of Music, and died here whilst on a visit to his son, who was headmaster of Taunton Grammar School.

Bishops Lydeard, the Almshouses

Bishops Lydeard

Described in an 1856 guidebook as 'a village coloured blood red by the soil', and pleasantly situated in the Vale of Taunton, Bishops Lydeard is a trim village of stone and thatched cottages. The almshouses dating from 1616 are much restored, but retain their mullioned windows, and to the north west of the church is the gracious mid 18th century Lydeard House.

The church has a fine, 16th century fan vaulted screen, an octagonal font and beautifully carved bench ends, depicting aspects of Somerset life including a stag, a miller and a ship. This superb red, sandstone church is particularly noted for its Perpendicular tower with four storeys surmounted by a pierced parapet, acknowledged to be one of the finest in Somerset. Also of interest is the 14th century cross with its richly sculptured socket and shaft. The almshouses of 1616 are much restored (*see also* Cothelstone).

The West Somerset Railway, Britain's longest privately preserved railway now operates again between Minehead and Bishops Lydeard, and the line still links with the British Rail tracks at Norton

Fitzwarren. A service operates between March and September, with a number of special events to capture the imagination of the general public as well as rail enthusiasts.

Taunton Model Railway Group functions in specially acquired premises on the station campus here.

Bishopswood, *see* Buckland St Mary

Blue Anchor, *see* Carhampton

Bossington

The charming hamlet of Bossington to the north east of Porlock has changed very little since an early guidebook described it as having a swift stream, rude old cottages, and antique walnut trees set against a background of 'the hillside with its patches of fern, its purple gullies of stones, its dark green furze crofts and waving woods.' Not surprisingly it has long been the haunt of artists and walkers.

There are superb walks all around this beautiful area, much of which is in the care of the National Trust. There are magnificent views from vantage points, particularly from the top of Bossington Hill. Descending to the coast at Hurlstone Point is Gull Hole, a large, natural arch. Hurlstone Point is said to have acquired its name because the Devil supposedly stood here to hurl large stones across the valley to Porlock Hill, although the reason for him indulging in this target practice is unclear. A slight variation on the same theme is that the Devil challenged an angel to a boulder slinging match — which the angel won; the two stones projecting from the heather at Whitestones providing evidence for the whimsical theory.

For those unable to cope with hill walking, there is a pleasant level mile long walk along the lane to Allerford, with its handsome walnut trees, delightful cottages and fine packhorse bridge.

Bradford-on-Tone

North of the A38 between Wellington and Taunton is the village of Bradford-on-Tone, which was once known as 'Bradeford', indicating a broad ford over the River Tone. Gradually this name mellowed with local tongues into 'Bradford', and the 'on-Tone' directional indication was added about a hundred years ago.

In 721 A.D. the manor passed to the De Montacues and later went to the Warres of Hestercombe. At the time of Domesday there was 'a mill of ten shillings rent and thirty acres of meadow and ten acres of pasture and seventy two acres of wood.' At one time cattle markets were held at Easter and in November.

The church of St Giles dates from about 1300, but contains mostly 14th and 15th century work. The tenor bell, dating from 1520 is reputed to be the finest in the county. The two arched bridge over the river, thought to be 15th century, was repaired in 1698 and is now protected as an ancient monument.

On the other side of the A38 is the much expanded village of Trull, reputed to have the finest ancient oak carvings of any church in West Somerset, and where children's writer Mrs Juliana Ewing was buried beneath a spreading yew tree.

Bratton Seymour

The crossroads at Bratton Seymour bear the name *Jack White's Gibbet*, and therein hangs a tale. Apparently a traveller staying at a Castle Cary inn was robbed and murdered, and Jack White was the principal suspect because he was reluctant to submit to the 'trial by touch' ordeal. Other suspects who agreed to the test by touching the corpse met with no reaction, but when Jack White finally agreed to do so a slight trickle of blood issued from the corpse's mouth and he was promptly arrested. Further investigations at Jack's place of work revealed a hoard of Spanish coins and the murdered man's Bible, inscribed with his name, William White. For the victim was none other than Jack's brother William, who had gone to sea to seek his fortune some years previously. In 1729 the murderer was suspended from the gibbet at the crossroads which still bear his name.

In 1882 Dr Brine told Thomas Hardy that the gibbet was there as recently as 1835 with the 'iron arm sticking out, and a portion of the cage in which the body had formerly hung'. The gibbet was destroyed by youngsters who piled faggots around it to create a big blaze one Guy Fawkes Night. Now an established part of local folklore, the story has been the inspiration for features, poems and plays which have been performed periodically in the area.

The River Cam, which rises between here and Yarlington, flows on through countryside of Arthurian legend characterised by gentle green hills and fertile valleys.

Brean

The limestone ridge of the Mendips stretches over twenty miles westwards from Frome and Shepton Mallet to Uphill, and beyond their western tip rise the isolated hills of Banwell, Bleadon, then the promontory of Brean Down with Steep Holm and Flat Holm as their Severn Estuary outposts.

Brean Down, with its ancient field systems and ruined Victorian fort is now in the care of the National Trust. It is exhilarating to walk on the springy turf, savour the breathtaking views and enjoy the wild flowers. Brean Down is important for its bird life and botanical interest, and is watched over by the Somerset Trust for Nature Conservation. Samphire, a much valued plant used for pickling, became a victim of overgathering in the days before conservation was understood. From the vantage point of Brean Down, the effect of Bristol Channel's huge tides along a flat coastline, leaving miles of gleaming sands, can be fully appreciated. Offshore, the Berrow flats carry prairies of *Spartina* grass, which trap mud and build up new marshland. It was described by the Rev William Greswell, an historian of earlier this century, as 'An amphibious region where nevertheless, man at certain times can neither creep, crawl, walk or swim, and the catastrophe of death follows the fisherman or shrimper who ventures carelessly on it in the half lights of a winter's afternoon.'

In St Bridget's churchyard are the graves of unfortunate sailors who fell victim to the treacherous Brean Sands, while the stonework shows evidence of having weathered many a storm.

Brendon Hill, *see* Luxborough and Clatworthy

Brent Knoll

Brent Knoll

The isolated hill known as Brent Knoll, capped with an Iron Age fort, rises abruptly and dramatically out of the central plain to a height of 450 feet. It is a familiar landmark for motorists on the A38 and M5 and for many miles around, and is one of the finest vantage points in Somerset — with views across to South Wales, Steep Holm and Flat Holm and miles of beautiful countryside. The name is thought to be derived from the Saxon 'Brennan' — meaning to burn — a possible allusion to the lighting of beacon fires to warn of impending dangers, and it may well have been a place of refuge during the Danish invasions of the 9th century. In AD 845 the menfolk of Somerset and Dorset joined together to defeat the warring Danes, and Battleborough, under the southern flank of the knoll, may well have been named in commemoration of the battle.

In a county steeped in history, with varied and dramatic contrasts, it is hardly surprising if legends surround the facts and offer explanations for the seemingly inexplicable. How did this unlikely knoll come to find itself in splendid isolation among Somerset's central plains? The Devil tossed up a spadeful of earth as he was busy digging the Cheddar Gorge — of course — how else? Another explanation — rather more scientific — is that the Somerset plain is penetrated by ridges and dotted with isolated hills capped by hard limestone, left when the rivers cut through the underlying soft clay. Thus Brent Knoll is the last remnant of a ridge between the Axe and Whitelake valleys, with a hard hat of limestone, and steep, sometimes slumping slopes in Lower Lias clay.

The village at its foot, known as Brent Knoll or South Brent, together with East Brent and Lympsham were part of the Glastonbury Abbey estate, and the church of St Michael, beautifully situated on the hillside with its Norman doorway and carved oak roof, re-echoes past monastic themes in a satirical way in its bench end carvings. It seems that a medieval abbot of Glastonbury had intentions of seizing parish revenue from the priest, while the priest and his parishioners were determined to hang on to it, and the ensuing ecclesiastical squabble was carved out by a local craftsman for posterity. In cartoon-like sequence, the abbot, depicted as a wily fox with pig and monkey headed minions, dominates innocent groups of animals and a flock of geese. The tables are turned; he is placed in the stocks and later hanged, with triumphant geese enthusiastically pulling at the noose.

Brompton Regis

The village, also known as King's Brompton, was originally named 'Brunan tun', indicating an enclosure by the Brendon Hills. This once off-the-beaten-track place, situated to the north east of Dulverton amongst steep hills was accessible only through narrow lanes.

The story goes that after escaping from the siege of Exeter in 1068, Ghida, the mother of King Harold refused to surrender Brunan tun to William the Conqueror's troops, and that she was allowed to stay on in her manor house under a type of house arrest arrangement until her death, when the manor and its little Saxon church were swept away.

In 1978 the modern 161 feet high dam on the Haddeo river began feeding the man-made lake known as Wimbleball Reservoir supplying water to parts of Somerset and Devon. Wimbleball Lake is now a recreational area with car parks, picnic sites and play areas. There is a nature reserve and walks and bridlepaths to be enjoyed. In addition there are facilities for club sailing, fishing and camping.

Broomfield

Andrew Crosse (1784-1855), the philosopher, who spent most of his time carrying out experiments with new fangled electricity at his Fyne Court home at Broomfield on the Quantocks, was regarded with suspicion and even suspected of being a wizard by some of his neighbours; a situation to become all the more eerie on account of his achieving the rare distinction of being born — and dying — in the same room. However, Sir John Trevelyan of Nettlecombe valued his work and Sir Humphry Davy and other scientists took an interest in his experiments.

The home of pioneer electrician Andrew Crosse has been demolished, but Fyne Court, now in the care of the National Trust, is the present headquarters of the Somerset Trust for Nature Conservation and information centre for the Quantocks.

Amidst a Quantock timber belt is the Iron Age Ruborough Camp, and from the hilltops there are breathtaking views across the Vale of Taunton Deane.

Brympton D'Evercy

The area around Yeovil and Chard is particularly well endowed with fine country estates and Brympton D'Evercy, near Yeovil, is generally acknowledged to be one of Somerset's showpieces, with its 15th century manor house, dower house, church, stables and gardens pleasingly arranged. Brympton House has a sculptured and battlemented west front and magnificent Palladian south wing. The low, 13th century church has a large bell cote over the west gable, and inside there are examples of 14th century stained glass, a 15th century stone rood screen and some interesting monuments.

Brympton D'Evercy derived its name from the family who were lords of the manor in the 13th century. It was later in the possession of the Stourton, Sydenham and Fane families. Situated in a fertile area on the Yeovil Sands, wheat was the most extensively grown crop in the 14th century, with some oats, peas and beans. Sheep and cattle were kept and oxen were used for ploughing. Tenant farmers, cottagers and peasant families lived on the manor.

Brympton D'Evercy House

Buckland Dinham

On the broken edge of the Mendip country, to the north west of Frome and set on a steep hillside, Buckland Denham or Dinham was a once busy town with a flourishing cloth trade, having received its charter from Henry III. The place owed much of its early importance to the Dinham family who arrived at the time of William the Conqueror.

The church, which has a Norman font and a 13th century chancel, has a 15th century tower, reckoned to be one of the finest in Somerset.

Upstream from Buckland Dinham, the little village of Hardington has a small church set amongst farm buildings containing a 17th century monument to Colonel Warwick Bampfield. The stables of the manor house are thought to be Georgian.

Buckland St Mary

This little village, 700 feet up in the beautiful Blackdown Hills west of Ilminster, and the nearest to Castle Neroche (*see* Staple Fitzpaine and Corfe), has an unusually large church, richly embellished with carvings of saints, apostles and angels. Opposite the church is the attractive school, constructed in similar grey stone. Country children shout and play in the freedom of their playground, in an open situation which must be the envy of city folk who chance to stray this way. The old fashioned advertisements displayed outside the post office still seem to be in keeping with the charming atmosphere of a village which has not changed all that much over the years. The Silver Jubilee Seat by the tall lych gate of St Mary's offers a suitable opportunity to sit in quiet contemplation *(see also* Pitminster*)*.

Castle Neroche, situated in a dominating, strategic position, was probably built on the site of an earlier fortification, for it is thought that the outermost of the earth ramparts was built by the Saxons, with further additions by the Normans. The outer bank rises sharply about 15 feet; the second bank towers another 15 or 20 feet above that, while the inner rampart rears another 25 feet. A narrow causeway leading to the motte is known as the Beacon. Castle Neroche Farm, rather unexpectedly situated amongst those ancient ramparts, has been in existence for about 200 years.

Today this leafy, delightful vantage point is administered by the Forestry Commission, who have set up a splendid Forest Trail which begins and ends in the car park set amongst the trees at nearby Castle Neroche.

Toll Bar Cottage, the 19th century toll house for the Honiton and Ilminster Turnpike Trust is situated at the cross roads above Bishopswood Bridge. The Candlelight Inn at Bishopswood was formerly the New Inn, and dates from the 17th century.

Burrowbridge

There are good views from the isolated Burrow Mump, a nine acre hill near Burrowbridge now in the care of the National Trust, where there is an unfinished late 18th century chapel, built on the site of an earlier one. There was formerly a small Norman castle here. Today Burrow Mump also commemorates 'The Men and Women of

Burrowbridge, Burrow Mump

Somerset who gave their lives in The Second World War.'

It was at Burrow Mump that King Alfred made his fort during the winter of 878, and planned his campaign to defeat the warring Danes under their leader Guthrum, thereby altering the course of our country's history *(see* Athelney*)*.

Burrowbridge, where the river Tone joins the Parrett, is the only bridge over the Parrett between Bridgwater and Langport and can be regarded as the gateway to Sedgemoor. The old three arched stone bridge at Burrowbridge, with deep cutwaters and pointed arches, was removed in the 1820s and replaced by a handsome, single arched structure in 1826. This was the last tollbridge in Somerset, having been freed in 1946.

This part of Somerset depended on waterborne trade until the coming of the railway in 1853, and Burrowbridge was a river port through which barges, carrying mostly coal, but also such things as iron, pitch, flax and wine made their way to Ham Mills and Taunton. Another tradition of the locality, the growing of withies for basket making is carried on, and the sight of the graceful willow shoots swaying in the breeze adds to the charm of this distinctive landscape.

Burton Pynsent Column, *see* Curry Rivel

Butleigh

Set in lovely countryside on the wooded slopes above Baltonsborough and south of Glastonbury, the village of Butleigh has distinguished Naval connections, for several of the famous Hood family were born here; a situation reflected in the church where there are a number of memorials including an epitaph written by the poet Southey. The two sons of the vicar, the Rev Samuel Hood, both went to sea, achieved great distinction and were created peers. The elder boy, born in 1724 and also named Samuel entered the Navy as a midshipman at the age of sixteen and became a rear admiral and was created Viscount Hood, while his brother Alexander, two years younger, became Commander of the Channel Fleet and later Lord Bridport (*see* Cricket St Thomas). Butleigh column, a well known landmark for miles around, of simple Roman Doric style, surmounted by nautical symbols and a naval crown honours Vice Admiral Sir Samuel Hood, one of their kinsmen, who was 'an officer of the highest distinction amongst the illustrious men who rendered their own age the brightest period in the naval history of their country.'

Butleigh was also the home of Neville Grenville, a squire who loved engines and mechanical things and was one of the first people to own a motor car.

The place is justifiably proud of its fine trees, which are particularly enchanting in springtime and in the autumn. The gardens of Butleigh are graced with some interesting species, including a thorn tree, said to bloom at Christmas, having been taken from St Joseph's Thorn at Glastonbury (*see also* Whitestaunton).

Cannington

Somerset County Council's Farm Institute at Cannington near Bridgwater now occupies the site of a 12th century Benedictine nunnery, which was dissolved in 1536 and re-established in 1807. An impressive, domed polygonal chapel, built in 1830 now serves as a hall of assembly for today's college students (*see also* Combe Florey).

The manor has been in the possession of the Clifford family for centuries, and the story goes that 'Fair Rosamund' (Rosamund Clifford) was born here and brought up with the young Henry II who fell in love with her and that they secretly married. In the cause of duty Henry was obliged to marry the forceful Eleanor, 'by the Wrath of God, Queen', and the divorced wife of the King of France. Rosamund was installed in a love nest at his palace and all went well until Eleanor spied a silken threat attached to her husband's spur as he emerged from the maze, and further investigations led to the fair Rosamund languishing in her bower. She was promptly packed off to this nunnery for the remainder of her days.

Gurney Street Farm, an old manor house near the church, has a tiny domestic chapel which is surmounted by a priest's chamber. On high ground above the village to the north west is an Iron Age earthwork known as Cynwit's Castle, scene of one of Alfred's battles with the Danes in 878.

John Pym, acknowledged to be a celebrated rebel — or a distinguished Parliamentarian — was born at Brymore House in 1584 and educated at Oxford. He was cited as 'the founder of party government in England'.

Caractacus Stone, *see* **Winsford**

Carhampton

Deep-rooted in tradition, the age old custom of wassailing is still observed on the Old Twelfth Night (16th January) at Carhampton, about five miles to the south east of Minehead. 'Wassail' means 'good health', and in the ceremony the trees are assured of our respect and empathy. Bonfires, the eating of toast and apples soaked in cider and the drinking of cider are symbolic actions to toast the spirit of the trees, thereby ensuring a good crop the following year. The Wassail Queen, carried aloft by strong, fresh complexioned Somerset lads would perform the sacramental act of sharing toast and cider with the best tree in the orchard by wedging toasted bread into the branches and dousing it with cider from an earthenware pitcher. Cheers, singing and intermittent loud noises would all serve to add to the atmosphere of the occasion and keep the tree spirits alert as to what was going on.

The climax was a rendition of:

'Old Apple Tree,
Old Apple Tree,
We wassail thee,
And hoping thou wilt bear.
For the Lord doth know

Where we shall be
'Till apples come another year,
For to bear well
And to bloom well.
So merry let us be.
Let every man
Take off his hat
And shout to thee
Old Apple Tree,
Old Apple Tree,
To wassail thee.
And hoping thou wilt bear
Hat fulls, cap fulls,
Three bushel bag fulls,
And a little heap
Under the stairs!'

There were a number of variations on this theme.

To the north is the former hamlet of Blue Anchor, with a wide expanse of sand and a number of caravans and facilities of a modern day resort. The West Somerset Railway re-opened as a private venture in 1976, operating initially between Minehead and here, but it now extends as far as Bishops Lydeard. Blue Anchor is the home of a Great Western Railway Museum.

Castle Neroche, *see* Buckland St Mary, Corfe and Staple Fitzpaine

Catcott

The main expanse of the Somerset moors is sharply bisected by the Poldens, which slope gently on their northern side where Catcott and a string of peat villages lie. Catcott is on the course of an ancient trackway dating from almost 3,000 years before the birth of Christ.

The quaint, 13th century church, which has no aisle or chancel arch, has plain, solid oak seats and a basic 13th century font. Inscribed on the walls are the Lord's Prayer, and a sermon from Titus in the form of a homily.

Catcott Heath, only 10 feet above sea level, is an area of outstanding botanical interest, closely watched over by Conservation groups. Until comparatively recent times some local folk lived in single storey mud and reed dwellings. The cottages seen on the moor today are mostly constructed of Bridgwater brick, and lack the elegant proportions of the stone cottages up in the hills.

Of even lesser substance is the ghostly funeral procession, thought to relate to some noteworthy individual, with coffin bearers on foot and mourners who appear near a dip in the road on the Shapwick side and wend their eerie way to the Quaker cemetery. There have also been reports of ghostly horses from the days of the horse carriages of the 18th or early 19th centuries rearing and shying, but whether this is connected with the funereal ghosts is not clear. A headless man, said to be the Duke of Monmouth, haunts a house in Churchyard Field where Monmouth is reputed to have stayed just before the Battle of Sedgemoor. A headless figure is seen to walk a field between here and Edington (*see also* Muchelney) .

Chaffcombe

The parish of Chaffcombe, bordered by Knowle St Giles, Cricket Malherbie, Cudworth, Cricket St Thomas, Winsham and Chard, occupies the western slopes of evocatively named Windwhistle Ridge on steep terrain overlooking Chard, which shelves away towards the old reservoir. The village, centrally placed in the parish, enjoys a peaceful, streamside situation in a sheltered valley between converging prongs of the hectic modern day A30 and A358. There is a seemingly haphazard network of tortuous, circuitous roads, directly evolved from lanes linking the old pattern of enclosures across the difficult terrain, and in the 11th century the settlements were probably widely scattered throughout the area.

Houses along the village street are mainly 18th and 19th century with modern development filling some of the gaps between. Although agriculture was the chief source of livelihood, there were close links with the cloth making and glovemaking industries based on factories at Chard and Ilminster.

Back in 1754 a schoolmaster was employed to teach children to write; at the beginning of the last century 30-40 children were taught at a Sunday School, which by the middle of that century had salaried teachers paid by the rector. The village school was built two years after the formation of a School Board in 1876 and was described in 1903 as being 'in good order and very well taught.' The school, later known as Chaffcombe County Junior School closed in 1959 at the beginning of a trend to cut costs and 'bus' children to neighbouring places.

Charlinch, *see* Spaxton

Charlton Mackrell

Modern day diesel locomotives thunder through the village of Charlton Mackrell to the east of Somerton, which found itself on the map in the earliest times; for the landscape, rich in archaelogical remains, bears evidence of at least five Roman buildings nearby as well as the important Roman thoroughfare known as the Fosse Way.

The church at Charlton Mackrell was where many of the Lytes family of Lytes Cary were buried. The family is thought to have settled at Lytes Cary in the middle of the 13th century. Henry Lyte, 'a most excellent scholar in several sorts of learning', produced one of the earliest works on scientific botany to be published in this country and established a botanical garden at Lytes Cary described by a later kinsman as 'a pretty good collection of plants for that age.' Henry Lyte was also the author of *The Light of Britayne; a Recorde of the honorable Orignall and Antiquitie of Britaine,* which he dedicated to Queen Elizabeth and presented to her in 1588 during thanksgiving festivities following the defeat of the Armada. Other members of the family followed an academic bent, producing works on geneology, history, antiquities and arithmetic, while the Rev Henry Francis Lyte wrote hymns.

Lytes Cary manor house, with its 14th century chapel, 15th century hall and 16th century great chamber, home to the Lyte family for over 500 years, is now run by the National Trust and open to the public. There is an ancient dovecote in the 365 acre grounds.

The River Cary meanders from Charlton Mackrell and Lytes Cary, past the small village of Kingsdon, on a hill to the western side. In the church at Kingsdon is a 13th century effigy of an armed knight, thought to be Guy de Briene, to whom Edward III gave the manor of Kingsdon.

Charterhouse

The lead ore to be found in the Mendips was exploited before the Romans came, and their knowledge of this wealth in the hills was an added incentive to invade. Charterhouse became the main area of Roman mining activity. All around is evidence of prehistoric life and close by is a Roman settlement and ampitheatre. Leaden sheets used in the Roman bath at Bath were excavated from here, and further information about their mining activities can be found in the museums in Bristol and Taunton.

The place got its name in the 13th century when the Carthusians of Witham created a cell here; for in 1283 they were granted a permit to work the lead mines *(see* Witham Friary*)*. Lead mining continued until around 1830.

Traditionally, the story goes, a man dug a hole waist deep, stood in it and flung his tools in opposite directions to stake his claim. The territory then became his 'groove' or 'gruffy.' The uneven, hummocky land still in evidence today, and difficult to cultivate, is the result of this 'gruffy ground' activity. Wild tales were told of the exploits of the lawless Mendip groovers, who were required to obtain licenses from the 'Lord Royal' of their particular area. For the mining areas were anciently divided into four sections, controlled by Lords Royal of Mendip, who took 10 per cent of the lead and administered claims at special courts. The reeves sorted out — and quite often created — disputes.

The 17th century Manor Farm is thought to have been built on the site of the Carthusian monastery. The church is quite recent, having been built in 1908. Dedicated to St Hugh, it was considered remote enough to have incorporated two fireplaces and a scullery in its building, which was most unusual.

Cheddar

The Mendip plateau rises to its highest point (1,068 feet) about 3 miles to the north of Cheddar, which lies along its sheltered, southern escarpment just to the south east of Axbridge. Early strawberries, anemones and other crops do well here, but of course Cheddar has long been synonymous with caves and cheese.

Back in the 16th century William Camden wrote of the place being 'famous for the excellent and prodigious cheeses made there, some of which require more than a man's strength to set them on the table.' Daniel Defoe, who visited the area in 1722 described the dairying methods and cheese making process, and declared Cheddar Cheese to be 'the best cheese that England affords, if not, that the whole world affords.'

Cheddar Caves are the best known of a large number of caves around the area. Gough's Cave is one of several known to have been inhabited by Upper Palaeolithic Man between 12,000 and 8,000 BC, and later occupied in the Iron Age and in Romano-British times. Described today as 'Britain's finest showcaves', the well lit, easy paths lead tourists through a labyrinth of passages and chambers with their still pools and fantastic stalactites and stalagmites. The museum houses many fascinating exhibits, including the famous skeleton of Cheddar Man. Cheddar Gorge, just outside the village attracts the wonder of many tourists, but is of particular scientific interest to geologists and botanists.

Also of interest is the lofty towered, mainly 14th century church of St Andrew, a market cross restored in 1887, the remains of a chapel belonging to Manor Farm, and the early Victorian red brick Court House, just to the south of the cross. Attracting the well heeled, who came here to look and marvel in Victorian times, the place is amply geared to the needs of tourists.

Chewton Mendip

The distinctive pinnacles of the superb 126 foot high church tower, acknowledged to be one of the very finest in the county, project proudly from the south east Mendip hillside, to be observed from afar. Like others of a similar style, it reflects a period of revived prosperity, when Somerset's wool exports were thriving.

There is much evidence of prehistoric importance, with a long barrow nearby and a cluster of Bronze Age barrows. In medieval times, this was part of a Royal hunting ground, where the kings had exclusive rights to the deer and wildlife, leaving humble villagers to exist as best they could, paying heavily for rights to graze and gather wood. For them, survival was difficult and poaching was a way of life entailing severe penalties. The lead mining potential, exploited from earliest times, was developed by the Romans *(see* Charterhouse*)*.

In the 19th century the ancient Waldegrave family contributed much to the area, and Countess Waldegrave was concerned about the housing and welfare of employee miners. Chewton Priory, built on the site of an earlier monastery is where Edward Lear, the author of nonsense verse stayed. His lively correspondence with Lady Waldegrave brimmed over with whimsical ideas and bizarre humour.

Beside the Wells to Bath and Bristol road is a large statue of Romulus and Remus, legendary founders of Rome being suckled by a she-wolf. This was the work of an Italian prisoner of the Second World War, who chose to stay on when the war ended and to make his home in Chewton Mendip.

Chilcompton

Rising near Old Down, a small tributary of the River Somer cascades its way through the charming little village of Chilcompton, to the north of Shepton Mallett, where the restored church has a 15th century tower, but contains little of antiquity. However, Darby and Joan of Chilcompton, who reached the ages of 95 and 88 respectively, presented three windows to the church on the occasion of Darby's attaining his 91st year.

Chillington

The parish of Chillington covers a triangular area on the northern slopes of the evocatively named Windwhistle Ridge. Like the neighbouring parish of Chaffcombe, it is characterised by steep terrain and combes, with a network of narrow lanes connecting ancient enclosures which seem today to be going nowhere in particular. With the Fosse Way running close by, there have been a number of interesting Roman finds around the area.

There is a Higher Chillington and a Lower Chillington. Lower Chillington, with its church, old manor house and two large farms and former cottages was regarded as the more important settlement, but by the 1970s, Higher Chillington had absorbed a larger population. The once arable land around Chibley Farm to the north west of the village was developed into water meadows in the middle of the 18th century. Butter from these farms was transported annually to Weymouth. The gradients supported cattle and sheep, but wheat, barley, flax, oats, beans and potatoes were also produced in early times. The emphasis switched to dairying in the 19th century when local cheese was sold, and dairying remains the mainstay of the area. At that time women and girls were also employed in glove making as a cottage industry, but the country folk were poor and they drifted away from the area leaving cottages empty when glovemaking fell into decline.

The Quaker preacher Elias Osborn (1643-1720), was born here, and in the late 17th century two Quakers were imprisoned for refusing to pay tithes. In the first part of the 19th century local children paid ½d a week to attend the Sunday School. The village school, established around the 1840's was closed in 1971, and its pupils transferred to Ilminster.

Chilthorne Domer

Roman roads run to the east and west of this village near Yeovil, while the site of a Roman villa lies to the south. The 13th century church, with its bell-cote instead of a tower, rather like those of Brympton and Ashington, has a 13th century monument to a knight in chain mail, thought to be Sir William Domer, who gave his name to the village. There is also a 15th century font and a Jacobean pulpit dated 1634.

Chilton Cantelo

About five miles to the north of Yeovil, between the river Yeo and Hornsey Brook lies the little village of Chilton Cantelo; its name thought to have been derived from the Cantilupe family.

In the churchyard lie the headless remains of Theophilous Broome, who died in 1670. As a staunch Parliamentarian during the Civil War, this Warwickshire man felt that Somerset was a pleasant place for retirement, but feared that retribution might catch up with him in death by the placing of his head upon a spike. So to prevent any possibility of this, he instructed his sister to bury his body but to keep his head in a safe place. She duly carried out these wishes and kept his head safely in an oaken cupboard at Higher Farm. Subsequent attempts to reunite his head with his body or to disturb it in any way have met with heartrending cries from the skull and bad luck for the occupants of the house.

Chilton Polden

Chilton Polden is one of a line of villages nestling along the northern slopes of the Poldens looking down over the peat moors. In this dappled setting, buildings and walls constructed from local stone are mellowed with lichen and age, and the air is alive with birdsong.

It was one of the 'Seven Sister' Polden villages which had close connections with the monks of Glastonbury, and the local wells, providing water rich in mineral salts, had healing qualities and were regarded as holy wells. Today few know the location of Chilton's well, which is overgrown and in a state of disrepair.

The ridgeway above Chilton Polden provides one of Somerset's finest vantage points, with views across the Mendips, Brent Knoll, the moorland, the Blackdowns and the Quantocks.

There is an old Polden Hills Shrove Tuesday custom whereby the mid-day ringing of the church bells was the signal for women to rush from their cottages clattering and banging pots and pans, crying 'Pan! Pan! Pan!' Children, who were given a half holiday would parade through the streets singing:

'Shrove Tuesday, Shrove Tuesday,
When Jack went to plough
His mother made pancakes,
She did not know how.
She tissed them,
She tossed them,
She made them so black
She put so much pepper
She poisoned poor Jack. Hooray!'

Churchingford

Six roads converge in perfect symmetry, like spokes linking with their supporting hub, all indicating that one of Somerset's delightful, lesser-known haunts was once important.

In Roman times it was the crossing point of the Fosse and Icknield thoroughfares and until comparatively recently it was a part of Devonshire. It was recorded that 'At Churchen ford (where stands not above a house or two) is kept a great yearly fair, on the feast day of St Paul.' At the ford (now a concrete bridge) stands an ancient mill, while the cottages and inn date from the 15th and 16th centuries. During renovations a priest's chamber containing a sword was discovered in the York Inn, and a Cromwellian sword was found at the post office.

According to legend, there was formerly a vast settlement on the Blackdowns, known as the 'City of Ford' or Cityford, with Churchingford being the site of its greatest church and Hemyock Castle its western fortification. The city was supposedly destroyed in a great war, after which its gates were carted off in triumph to France. Vast boulders which formerly lined the road from here to Hemyock were thought to have come from the city, and were treated with great respect by local folk who attributed mystical properties to them.

Out on the surrounding moorlands it was said that a pale apparition, which rose at midnight, floated towards lonely travellers rustling eerily, an outstretched bony claw pointing a long talon at the stranger's heart. Not surprisingly, this would cause the unfortunate person to take leave of his senses. If the spirit went so far as to lay a white, clammy hand on his heart, it was instant death for the victim, with the white digital imprint left on the corpse for all to see. However, one intrepid farmer put an end to his nonsense once and for all. Armed with the rather unlikely defence of a hunk of bread and a fistful of salt, he ventured forth alone, just before the expected appearance. When the distant church clock chimed midnight, the apparition arose and floated eagerly towards the intended victim. However, the nimble farmer dodged the impending hand of doom and thrust the fistful of salty bread into the looming face in satisfying, traditional custard pie style. With a final crumpling sound the spirit vanished, never to be seen again.

Churchstanton

This place of quietness and unspoilt beauty in the Blackdown Hills, approached by a maze of secondary roads where strangers tend to lose their way, was a part of Devon until 1896. The name is thought to have been derived from Estanton, meaning Stony Town, and has a number of variations on that theme (*see* Churchingford). Nearby is an earth mound, thought to be the site of ancient worship.

Churchstanton is a large parish without very much of a village, and in earlier times the church of St Peter and St Paul drew its congregation from scattered settlements around the parish. Legend would tell us of a former large city nearby, which was totally destroyed by enemies who took the city gates as a trophy, and large blocks of stone found around the area, thought to have come from the buildings are said to possess magical or supernatural powers. Sinister events surround one such block of stone which came to be known as the Devil's Stone. A group of merrymakers returning from a party stopped by this stone and dared the Devil to emerge. When a gigantic, bellowing creature with horns appeared, they took to their heels and fled, with the creature in hot pursuit. It is said that it remained outside their locked door, bellowing until dawn.

This area, traditionally dependent on farming, suffered from low wages and large families. Some women found employment in local cloth mills, but the young men drifted towards the towns or joined the services. There was a silk factory at nearby Stapley, which had the advantage of exploiting cheap labour. Raw silk brought out from Taunton was spun and woven here. Stapley Mill, a former grist mill now converted into use as a private dwelling looks particularly enchanting amongst the leafiness and colour of late spring.

Clapton

About three miles to the south west of Crewkerne lies the little Axe Valley hamlet of Clapton, with its roadside mill, intriguingly named Blue Boy inn and Clapton Court — whose gardens are a delight to visitors. Clapton was one of the early valley settlements in the parish of Crewkerne, and there were documented references to the Blue Boy in 1780.

Clapton Court is a large, gabled house situated in well planted grounds which are frequently open to the public. The site of Clapton Manor House was probably occupied by the Clapton family in the 13th century and possibly earlier.

A mill was functioning here before 1228, and in 1263 the owner Walter Boce obtained the right to have the waters of the Axe diverted to drive his mill. Used as a corn mill in the 16th century, it was called Langdon's Mill in the middle of the 17th century and Lower Mill later in the same century. The present mill was built in 1875, and in recent times had three pairs of millstones, a roller mill and a cubing plant. A second mill held by Clapton Manor in the early 17th century was on the west side of the road through Clapton. When it ceased grinding in the last century it was converted to a farmhouse at Clapton Court and was referred to as Court Farm.

Clatworthy

The village of Clatworthy in the Brendon Hills has witnessed many changes, both ancient and modern. Up on the hill to the west of the village is Clatworthy Castle, an Iron Age camp roughly triangular in shape which formerly looked out across the young River Tone which rises on King's Brompton Common near Brendon Hill. Today, the man-made Clatworthy Reservoir, in its attractive setting, is an amenity area with picnic tables and a nature trail, offering visitors pleasing views across lake and woodland.

Clatworthy Reservoir, built in the late 1950s is one of a number of reservoirs constructed around the Somerset and Devon borderland to supply the growing needs of expanding country towns. Like the other reservoirs, it has matured into the landscape well and is the haunt of wildfowl.

The whitewashed church of St Mary has a plain west tower with diagonal buttresses and battlements. Inside the tower are three old bells, one dated 1699 and bearing the inscription 'Drawe neare to God.'

Combe Florey

This exceptionally pretty village off the main Taunton to Minehead road between the Brendons and the Quantocks, and set in a leafy combe, derived its name from the Florey family, ancient lords of the manor. Described by Edward Hutton as probably the loveliest village he had ever seen, it is a place of enchantment in an area which has traditionally been an inspiration to poets and writers.

Combe Florey was the home of wit, eccentric and unconventional cleric Sydney Smith, who, originally a lover of city life regarded the countryside as 'a kind of healthy grave,' soon changed his mind and declared that he was 'extremely pleased with Combe Florey' and pronounced it to be a very pretty place in a very beautiful county.' He continued to live here even after becoming canon of St Paul's Cathedral. He liked to delight, surprise and shock people and was a great practical joker. To fool his sophisticated London friends into believing how mild the climate was down Somerset way, he tied oranges onto the shrubs in the garden. When someone had commented that the sight of deer would add a touch of distinction to the rectory, he fixed antlers to his rather surprised pet donkeys. Sydney Smith had a spontaneous, witty epithet for every occasion, which broke the ice and melted barriers away. At first the villagers were somewhat bemused with this cheerful extrovert with his somewhat comical physical appearance, and of tales of strange goings-on at the rectory. But he very soon won their confidence and endeared himself to everyone, taking on unofficial roles as doctor, counsellor and magistrate, and living out his philosophy to 'Do good and be happy.' This lovable, unconventional vicar, described by Macauley as 'the greatest master of ridicule in England since Swift', is commemorated in the church's east window. The village was also the home of Evelyn Waugh, who lived here from 1956 until his death in 1966.

From much earlier times there is a bizarre incident concerning the Merriot family, for the wife of Sir John Merriot left her husband to become a nun of the Benedictine Priory at Cannington in the 13th century. When she died her husband wanted her laid to rest at Combe Florey, so that he could be buried beside her. When his request was refused he somehow managed to obtain her heart, and buried it here. But this act resulted in his being excommunicated from the church, and absolution only followed when he returned her heart.

Comberow, *see* **Gupworthy**

Combe St Nicholas

In the manner of a spider's web, seven lanes lead to this now peaceful village, spinning out from a network of encompassing lanes. For Combe St Nicholas, situated about five miles to the south east of Castle Neroche, lies in an area bearing evidence of intensive prehistoric activity, with Bronze Age barrows and the site of a Roman villa nearby. In 1070 the Manor of Combe was bought by Giso, Bishop of Wells.

Before the landing of the rebel Duke of Monmouth, rumours were rife throughout the local countryside, and a prediction overheard in a Wellington inn about the timing of the landing was enough to cause William Way of Combe St Nicholas to be promptly arrested. Appearing before the magistrate he earnestly pleaded that he was merely joking. Intelligence reports urged 'all honest Protestants forthwith prepare and make yourselves ready,' and when Monmouth landed at Lyme Regis in the late spring of 1685 supporters from Somerset, Devon and Dorset rushed to enlist.

In 1823 young Betty Trump took her last stroll along the lanes between Combe St Nicholas and Buckland St Mary, for the 14 year old girl was attacked, and having had her throat cut was dragged into a nearby wood, to be discovered several days later. A man who was thrust into prison was subsequently released, having been saved by another man's deathbed confession.

The Devil's Stone, which has now been destroyed, was one of the three stones in nearby villages which were reputed to mark the grave of Giant Gorme, who was said to have fought the Devil — and lost.

Modern day inhabitants take a pride in the village, and an array of daffodils around the little green make it a particular delight in spring. There are lovely views from the surrounding hilltops.

Combe Sydenham, ***see*** **Monksilver and Stogumber**

Combwich

'Cummidge', an ancient port on the tidal estuary of the River Parrett was one of Somerset's three main ports in the 15th century, the others being Axwater and Minehead. It traditionally had a ferry and was the crossing place for early pilgrims and travellers from Combwich to Pawlett Hams. In 1480 a Combwich vessel, the *Anne,* commanded by William Farieman plied between Minehead and Bristol, carrying fish, hides and cork. By Victorian times Combwich Farmers' Association had a small but busy fleet, much used by local yeomen, millers and maltsters. Bridgwater bricks were exported to the South West and Ireland, while coal was brought across from South Wales. Canadian timber ships anchoring in the reach discharged their cargoes overboard to be chained together and rafted upstream to Bridgwater or beyond. Thus the port of Combwich provided employment and was the home of 'hobblers', lightermen and others connected with shipping.

According to the nature of the local clay, bricks of the perforated style and tiles were produced here. Latterly, with stern competition from bigger companies, the emphasis shifted to hand made tiles.

The characteristic 'flatners', used by local fishermen, flat bottomed double ended craft resembling Newfoundland Banks dories, are used for reaching nets on the far side of the channel. The tide which flows up the Severn estuary becomes squeezed and contracted producing turbulent waves known as the Severn Bore. It also creates a similar, but less dramatic effect up the Parrett. Richard Warner, who crossed the Parrett from Combwich at the beginning of September 1799, recorded somewhat entertainingly: 'As I had been informed that the Parrett was remarkable for the impetuosity with which the tide enters its mouth, I waited about an hour and a half, till the commencement of the flood, in order to observe the phenomenon. Its approach is announced by a distant roaring sound, which gradually increases upon the ear, until the cause itself appears; a volume of water, like one vast wave, sometimes rising to the height of four feet (though when I saw it, not more than two) rushing on with irresistible violence, and covering instantaneously the steep banks, which had been left dry by the recess of the tide. It is called Boar, in allusion, I presume, to the formidable sounds which this indomitable animal emits . . . It has best known, when strengthened by spring tide, to have overturned large boats in its furious course.'

The filthy slime which every tide left behind had an unlikely potential, spotted in Victorian times to become a household word; for the scum, collected, baked into 'bricks' and dried in the sun, became the famous 'Bath bricks', used as a scouring agent here and abroad.

Times change. Modern chemicals have replaced 'Bath bricks', competition and changing technologies have affected the brick making industry, while the ancient port of Combwich silted up and fell into decline. However, with the coming of Hinkley Point Nuclear Power Station the small harbour was reconstructed so that material could be brought to the power station by sea.

Compton Dundon

Dominated by Dundon Hill, which is capped by a tumulus and an Iron Age fort in a remarkably good state of preservation, and situated between the sites of Roman villas, Compton Dundon to the south of Glastonbury, is made up of the hamlets of Compton, Dundon and Littleton, with the church being at Dundon. Compton contains some delightful, well restored old houses and the remains of a wayside cross. The church of St Andrew has an embattled tower, with a 14th century chancel and 15th century nave.

Up on the ridge to the north is the monument to Vice Admiral Sir Samuel Hood *(see* Butleigh*)*.

At Littleton Roman remains are scattered over a 30 acre site and the indications are that a fine Roman house with a mosaic floor was built over an earlier Roman construction, which occupied the sites of two earlier British buildings.

Compton Pauncefoot

Close to Cadbury Castle, in land of Arthurian legend, Compton Pauncefoot, with its attractive houses, duckpond, modern castle, rolling parkland and lake fed by the six wells of Sigwells, is regarded as one of the gems of east Somerset.

Set amidst leafiness, and framed on all sides by the gently rounded hills, the buildings are constructed of golden, greenish grey stone, pleasing to the eye. The unusual crescent of three storey buildings with latticed windows dating from the beginning of the last century served as dwellings for the workers.

Corfe

This Blackdown village on the course of the Broughton Brook lies 3 miles to the south of Taunton, with the 16th century Barton Grange just to the west of the village bordering Poundisford Park. It was a former hunting estate belonging to the Bishops of Winchester, who also held Taunton Castle.

The neat, well tended church of St Nicholas was reconstructed in 1844 in the Norman style, with the low, square tower replaced in 1858 by the present one which has a peal of four bells.

A number of roads around the Blackdown Hills have sinister reputations, and near Corfe the luckless traveller might come across a headless rider in a flying cloak astride a horse with silent hooves, or a female rider on a white steed who melts through the gates and obstacles along her route.

In the 18th century some 'hopefuls' of Corfe went in search of the legendary riches associated with Castle Neroche, which is about 3 miles to the south east, taking with them the local parson armed with salt and holy water, and arranging for the church bells to ring out as protection against the Devil, who reputedly guarded the treasure. Excavations began, and, as F.W. Mathews related in *Tales of the Blackdown Borderland:* 'One man struck a large stone, which on lifting out disclosed an iron bound trunk . . . the treasure chest! In his excitement he rapped out a most blasphemous oath, and immediately the trunk sand down down out of sight, the great hole it had occupied closed up, and no more was seen of the treasure. Disheartened, they left their tunnel, but came back to it next evening and for a few more times, but ill-fortune dogged them. One stubbed his hand on an old moot (tree stump), another had his foot crushed, and finally, one sultry evening when the whole air was tense with a brooding thunderstorm, their nerves gave way in panic, and with yells of terror, they dropped their tools, and in deadly fear scattered to the woods, to find their way later, a scared and trembling mob, to the village, where they could scarcely tell coherently what had happened, save that "there was devils up in the Mount, they know'd there was, cos they'd yer'd 'em and zeed 'em too." They nearly all took sick, some died in a raging fever, others recovered, but shaken and broken men; and all the band, through terrible accidents or lingering sickness were dead before the year was out.'

Today the pleasing village of Corfe on the edge of the green and wooded Blackdown Hills looks out over the Vale of Taunton towards the hills beyond. The Village Green, which was given to the Parishioners of Corfe on June 20th 1887 'in loving and grateful commemoration of the 50th anniversary of Queen Victoria's happy reign' is now a pleasant buttercup meadow with seats and swings for the young and old to enjoy.

Cossington

The old branch line linking Bridgwater with Glastonbury made its scenic way around Cossington, through Chilton Moor and Shapwick Heath, providing one of the best and most enjoyable ways of seeing the peatmoors and Poldens. Sadly, the line is now closed.

Cossington is the most easterly of a chain of four villages running along the northern side of the Polden range, and in common with those villages it has its own holy well *(see* Chilton Polden, Edington *and* Catcott*)*. The pretty village has a 13th century church and a Preaching Tree, so called because Wesley once stood beneath its shade to preach.

Across the course of the old Roman road, the little village of Bawdrip, clustered around its interesting little church looks out across Sedgemoor. As the road drops down to Woolavington there are delightful views of the Burnham Levels, Glastonbury, Brent Knoll and across to the Mendips. Beyond Woolavington and Puritan the Polden Hills give way to the lush pastures beside the Parrett estuary.

Cothay Manor, *see* Langford Budville

Cothelstone

On the southern Quantock slopes, the manor house, church, and a handful of cottages make up the village of Cothelstone which had an ancient well, thought by some to be a holy well and by others to be a wishing well with connections with pixies and pins.

The original manor house, which was very grand and partially destroyed during the Civil War, was the home of the Stawell family since the time of the Norman Conquest. Sir John Stawell, one of the King's most loyal supporters raised a small army at his own expense, with weapons reputedly stored in the church tower at Bishops Lydeard. He was to pay dearly for his principles, for he was imprisoned, his home was partially demolished, his forests were cut down and his lands were sold. He died shortly after the Restoration and Charles II conferred the title Baron Stawell on his son, Ralph. Colourful in death as well as in life, the eccentric Sir John planned his own extravagant funeral arrangements, including refreshment facilities along the processional way. He lies buried with other members of his family in a chapel dating from around 1200 in the church.

On Shrove Tuesday local schoolchildren traditionally paraded to the 'big farm' and neighbouring farms and cottages, where they were given apples, pennies and cakes, and they would sing:

> 'Dimmery, dimmery dinky do
> Give me a pancake and then I'll go.
> Off with the kettle and on with the pan
> Please put a pancake in my hand.'

Cothelstone, the Manor gatehouse

Cranmore, *see* Doulting

Creech St Michael

Ancient and modern routes converge around Creech St Michael, a village on the Tone just east of the county town of Taunton. Close to the motorway and to the main Paddington to Penzance line, where high speed trains slow down before stopping at Taunton, it is also near the point of the now disused branch line southwards to Chard Junction, and where the old Bridgwater and Taunton and Chard canals met. The Kennet and Avon Canal from London extended as far as Bath in 1810, with the Bridgwater and Taunton Canal opening in 1827. Competition from the railways hastened their decline and this system is now used mainly for drainage relief to prevent flooding on the Somerset Levels. The Chard Canal, which traversed the moorland country by aqueduct is now abandoned in a state of disrepair.

The pleasant village of Creech St Michael, at the head of one of the long arms of the great marsh, is framed by low, green hills; its fine church tower providing a familiar landmark for rail travellers.

Cricket Malherbie, *see* **Dowlish Wake**

Cricket St Thomas

Cricket St Thomas lies off the A30 between Crewkerne and Chard and is well known to holidaymakers for its wildlife park, which offers a pleasant family day out. The park at Cricket St Thomas with its lovely house also became familiar to millions of TV viewers as the location for the serial *To The Manor Born.*

For nearly six hundred years the nearby Purtington Brook was harnessed to work a succession of mills, including corn and grist mills, blade mills, tucking mills, fulling mills and saw mills. In 1635 miller Bryant Langley was killed by the fall of his mill wheel. In the 17th century the brook was adapted to create water meadows.

Originally the village of Cricket was situated on the slopes below Cricket House, but most folk left when their houses were cleared away in the early 19th century for the expansion of the new manor house and the improvement of its setting. The old manor house, which had three beer cellars, a large brewhouse and numerous chambers and garrets, was destroyed in the late 18th century.

A Whitsunday Fair was established on White Down in the 14th century and extended to a week-long event over the next three hundred years. The sale of cattle, horses, sheep and leather attracted buyers from neighbouring counties. By the 19th century there was horse racing, foot hurdle racing, wrestling, cudgel playing and a variety of other contests, but the event died out at the beginning of this century. In the 18th century, fine folk, well aware of the importance of mixing with their own class enjoyed a 'carriage day', with 'feasting and dancing on the green sward.'

In the 18th century the vestry supplied the poor with cakes and ale at Eastertime. They insisted that their own poor should occupy the poorhouse in the village and that outsiders should not be in receipt of their help. The poorhouse was demolished along with the rest of the village.

Cricket St Thomas was once the home of Alexander Hood who became Lord Bridport (1726-1814). A son of the vicar of Butleigh, he distinguished himself as a Naval commander and was elevated to the peerage. His brother, who similarly distinguished himself became an admiral and was created Viscount Hood *(see* Butleigh*)*.

In olden days the road between Crewkerne and Chard in the vicinity of Windwhistle Hill was said to be haunted by Customs men and smugglers chasing along on their steeds to an accompaniment of evocative sounds of shots and firing. There have been no recent reports; surely no self respecting spectre would court the hazards of modern day traffic whizzing along the busy A30?

Croscombe

An early guide book enthused: 'Croscombe is full of old houses and is one of the most charming villages in all this country.' This lovely Mendip village with its clear stream, narrow, winding lanes and pleasing stone built houses, situated in the well wooded valley between Shepton Mallet and Wells knew early importance, having been granted charters for a fair and market by Edward I. In common with Shepton Mallet and other nearby places, it was once very much concerned with the woollen trade, but as that trade lost out to the north of England, the emphasis shifted to the production of crêpe, silk and finely knitted hosiery.

The noble church, which has a spire instead of the more usual Somerset tower, is particularly interesting. It's interior contains richly carved woodwork in its roof, screen, pulpit and pews. Dating from the 13th century and rebuilt in the 15th century, it bears testimony to the local wealth then being generated by the woollen trade. The two storeyed vestry was the meeting place of the Seven Guilds of Croscombe, namely the Young Men, the Maidens, the Wives, the Archers, the Webbers, the Fullers and the Hogglers (labourers). What happened to the husbands? Could this be an early example of discrimination?

The inhabitants have always demonstrated their loyalty, individuality and independence. Towards the end of the 19th century when local waywards considered the village cross to be an obstacle which needed removing in the name of 'Progress', indignant villagers drove them away, unfurling and brandishing a flag proclaiming 'Be Faithful', which they just happened to have handy at the time. Warming to their cause, they lit a fire and encamped around the cross until it was established that they had won a victory in the face of this early threat of 'red tape'.

Today, local folk display a similar spirit and humour, and Croscombe Frolics Society performs the craziest antics on Boxing Day to amuse and entertain, thereby raising funds for worthwhile local causes.

Crowcombe

Nestling beneath the steep, wooded Quantock slopes this enchanting village with its thatched cottages and ancient church still retains an aura of bygone tranquillity. The delightful Quantock landscape, dissected by wooded combes, with heather clad hills where deer and ponies add to the pleasure of the walkers, whilst buzzards hover overhead.

Shortly before the Norman Conquest, Gytha, wife of Earl Godwin made a gift of the Manor to the monks of Winchester as an act of atonement on her husband's behalf in an effort to save his soul. Soon afterwards the Manor was seized by William the Conqueror and presented to the Earl of Morton. Godfrey de Crowcombe, a later Lord of the Manor witnessed the meeting between King John and the barons at Runnymede.

The church of the Holy Ghost formerly had a tower with a spire. However, the spire was struck by lightning in 1725 and crashed through the roof. Part of it was preserved in the churchyard. The carvings inside the church, considered by some to be unrivalled, depict a miscellany of traditional themes including birds and beasts, winged creatures and monsters, mermen and mermaids, medallions and geometric shapes and men grappling with dragons. In earlier times a handbell ringer went down the alleyway summoning good folk to church.

Across the road is the village hall, originally the Church House where holy bread was baked and holy ale was brewed. During the 17th century a school was housed in the upper storey, while the aged poor lived down below. Each storey had a separate owner, and when the roof fell into disrepair and the owner of the second storey approached his ground level counterpart with the suggestion that they co-operated financially in carrying out repair work, he must have been somewhat bemused to receive the answer that the owner of the lower section was actually considering pulling his part of the building down!

Crowcombe, Church House

Behind the church in an area of wooded parkland is Crowcombe Court, built between 1725 and 1736 and regarded as one of Somerset's architectural gems, being constructed of brick and Ham stone with Corinthian pillars and having superb proportions. In its former more glorious days one guest had the audacity to complain that the screaming of the resident peacocks which graced the immaculate lawns had interfered with his sleep. The building has now been taken over for other purposes.

Some former inhabitants seem reluctant to leave the place. The Elizabethan part of Crowcombe Rectory is haunted by a lady in a silvery blue dress and matching shoes, who, quiet and benign, appears only occasionally — and then only to children.

Up to the beginning of this century the Crowcombe Mummers blackened their faces and got themselves all decked out to visit surrounding villages at Christmas time and the New Year to re-enact the traditional, moral messages as in days of yore. Armed with kettledrums, triangles, concertinas and banjos, the performers set out, to return through the lanes in the wee small hours, just in time to start the day's work.

In this locality it was customary for folk to go a-wassailing around the orchards, offering cider to one and all and presenting it to the trees. Gunshots into the trees, combined with singing and dancing all helped to keep the tree spirits on their toes and encouraged them to work well towards the next harvest *(see* Carhampton*)*.

The West Somerset Railway, restored as a private venture in recent years, reaches its highest point at Crowcombe. This enchanting, scenic route offers an deal way to savour the Quantocks as well as tantalising glimpses of the sea between Minehead and Williton and the working harbour at Watchet. The station has won the West Somerset Best Kept Station Award several times, and in 1985 won a first class prize in the National Best Restored Station Competition organised by The Association of Railway Preservation Societies. As one of around 2,500 such stations in Britain, this was quite a feat, and a great distinction for the dedicated and hardworking folk who look after the station.

Cucklington

Close to the border with north Dorset, and lying about 3 miles to the east of Wincanton, this pleasant little village situated on a ridge above the Blackmoor Vale commands magnificent views across Somerset and Dorset. The road zigzags its way to the top of the hill where one can savour the effects of light and shade and scudding clouds across the romantic and beautiful Vale of Blackmoor, a landscape which inspired the writer Thomas Hardy. This flat valley, lying on the heavy Oxford Clay and formerly well wooded, was known as Selwood Forest.

The mostly 13th century church of St Lawrence, has a medieval window depicting the head of St Barbara, whose name was also used for the village well. St Aldhelm, who preached hereabouts adds another saintly touch to the area.

Cudworth

The winter winds roar around the northern scarp of Windwhistle ridge, described in the 18th century as 'an elevated and delightful spot'; a vantage point combining 'unbounded prospects of the surrounding country and the British and Bristol Channels'. It is said that the section of road between Chard and Crewkerne is haunted by Customs men and smugglers on horseback and that the atmosphere re-echoes the sound of phantom firing. In recent years a motorist and his wife were shocked when a tall, dark lady in a crinoline style dress wafted her stately way across the road into their headlight one summer's night; the driver braked suddenly and she disappeared without trace, leaving the occupants of the car shaken, but with a clear memory of her appearance.

Cudworth is situated almost north of Cricket St Thomas, between Chaffcombe and Chillington in an area intersected by brooks which flow to join the River Isle. It is also close to the Fosse Way, an old Roman road. In the early days woodland was cleared for the planting of crops, but some of the woodland remains on the higher slopes, just below Windwhistle Ridge.

In common with surrounding places the folk of Cudworth were engaged not only in agriculture, but in weaving, dressmaking, glovemaking and the production of sailcloth. The 12th century church of St Michael is built of ashlar and rubble. There was an inn in the parish, known in the 18th century as the Black Horse. By the end of that century records indicate that Windwhistle Inn on the north side of the Crewkerne to Chard road was in existence, although it later incorporated a 19th century building.

Culbone

'Culbone, Oare and Stoke Pero,
Three such places you'll seldom hear o' . . .

Culbone, Oare and Stoke Pero,
Parishes three, no parson'll go to.'

So said the old rhyme. Today it is the haunt of the more energetic visitors and walkers, who take the paths through the woods to get there, for no roads lead to Culbone. Situated on the clifftop just to the west of Porlock Weir, it has always been considered 'singularly romantic . . . placed like a nest in a nook of the coast', so the old guide books tell us, with a church 'situated in as extraordinary a spot as man in his whimsicality ever fixed on for a place of worship.' If the paths become slippery and the going gets tough these days, spare a thought for the moorland folk in former days who made their way from isolated farms to worship at the church. The church, said to be the earliest Christian site on Exmoor, is reputedly the smallest parish church in England still in regular use for worship.

Charcoal burning and oak felling were extensively carried out in Culbone Woods, and the original charcoal burners were thought to have been a colony of lepers who were forbidden to cross over Culbone Water to the Porlock side. Remains of these huts and old trackways linking the pits can still be seen, and in the church is a window reputed to be a Lepers' Window. Later charcoal burners bartered charcoal for food and other necessities of life and hunted wild goats. The need for charcoal declined when coal was used for iron smelting, and oak felling became uneconomic as iron replaced timber for shipbuilding.

Culbone Church

Curland

The strung out hamlet of Curland, in delightful countryside beneath Castle Neroche and about 1½ miles south of Staple Fitzpaine in the Blackdowns, is well worth exploring. From here there is a steep path up to Castle Neroche through the plantation *(see* Buckland St Mary*)*. This combines with a network of trackways and paths in an area interesting for its ecology, the beauty of its trees in the changing seasons and spectacular views from the higher slopes.

Curry Mallet

On a sudden escarpment to the south of West Sedge Moor, lies the village of Curry Mallet, one of several 'Curry' villages on rising land almost enclosing it, and named after the Mallet family who arrived here at the time of the Norman Conquest. The manor house which replaced the Norman castle, rebuilt in the 16th century is said to be haunted. The course of the old Chard Canal passed to the west of the village, while to the south east the Fivehead river flows to join the River Isle which merges with the Parrett near Muchelney.

Curry Rivel

The soil around Curry Rivel and Athelney has the ideal blend of moisture and alkalinity for the growing of withies, which are pollarded willows, used for the making of baskets and fish traps. The industry expanded in Victorian times, with the fashion for wicker-made furniture, but the market has declined in recent years. Withies can still be seen soaking in the rhines and drying in rows. In some parts they are planted in sets in February and harvested in the autumn, having reached a height of about 6 feet. The slim green and silvery shoots are a distinctive feature of the Somerset Levels. Red Hill, now in the care of the National Trust, offers an agreeable point from which to savour it all.

Curry Rivel, perched on a neck of rising land stretching across the marshes towards Langport, derived its name from the 12th century lord Sir Richard Rivel. Its mainly 15th century church, faced with Ham stone, has 13th century monuments and stained glass, and a scratch dial from the days prior to clocks.

The village has associations with William Pitt, Sir William Pynsent and Lady Hester Stanhope. Sir William Pynsent, an eccentric old gentleman who had fallen out with most of his family, was very impressed with Pitt, particularly as he was opposed to the cider tax. Despite several attempts to see his hero to voice his approval in person, the baronet's scruffy appearance led to his never getting past the politician's servants. Thus, on his death in 1765, he left most of his property to William Pitt, a man he had never actually met. Pitt, as an act of respect and appreciation employed 'Capability' Brown to design the 140 foot column, inscribed, 'Sacred to the memory of Sir William Pynsent,' and paid him £2,000 to do so. Today the Burton Pynsent Monument, colloquially known as Burton Steeple, with its doorway leading to a 175 stepped spiral staircase has a fine view from the top, is kept locked on account of inquisitive and determined cows who have ventured into the doorway and emerged at the top!

The talented Lady Hester Stanhope enjoyed riding about the countryside and making friends with the country folk. She kept house for William Pitt the Younger before demonstrating her individuality still further by retiring to the slopes of Mount Lebanon. She remained in touch with Somerset folk and sent gifts to the village.

Adjoining Curry Rivel and Drayton is the Elizabethan Midelney Manor. Behind it is an early 18th century Falcons' Mews, constructed of brick with stone dressings. Drayton's church of St Catherine, constructed of Lias and Ham Hill stone has a low, embattled west tower and possesses a 15th century churchyard cross. Traces of a Romano-British building were discovered at the vicarage, and there was a nearby Roman villa.

Cutcombe

The Exmoor parish of Cutcombe, incorporating Dunkery Beacon and qualifying as the highest in Somerset, contains much evidence of prehistoric activity, with Cutcombe Barrow lying about 4 miles to the south east of the village. Cutcombe, on secondary and unclassified roads lies just off the A396 near Wheddon Cross and commands stunning views over Exmoor and the Brendons.

The church, with its high, plain tower is mainly 14th and 15th century and has a Norman font. The south aisle was built in the 19th when iron mining in the Brendons generated wealth in the locality.

At Eastertide it was the custom to carry posies of primroses, catkins and violets to church. It was important to have all three varieties for they were symbolic: the violets being thought to attract good luck. It was also considered lucky to climb to the top of Dunkery Beacon and watch the Easter Day sunrise.

It is not surprising that an area so lonely and at the mercy of the elements is steeped in folklore and mystery. On the road from Cutcombe to Timberscombe a phantom, driverless hearse, drawn by four, black headless horses is reputed to have been responsible for many an accident around these parts. Also gruesome is the story of the 16 year girl, Mollie Phillips, who set out in 1929 to walk from the farm where she worked in Exford to visit her aunt in Cutcombe. She never arrived, but her remains were discovered in a bog at Codsend near Dunkery Beacon two years later. How she strayed so far from her intended route or what happened to her will remain a secret of Exmoor for ever.

Dinder

On the edge of the Mendip escarpment between Wells and Shepton Mallet lies the delightful village of Dinder, living up to the promise of its engaging rural name. For this peaceful place with its pleasant buildings, old church with a lych gate almost enveloped by yew trees, and little stream tumbling its way to join the River Sheppey, presents a perfect pastoral scene.

The church, with its 17th century stone pulpit, is mainly 15th century, but some Norman work remains. There are memorials to the Somerville family, including Admiral Sir James Somerville, who had a distinguished career in the last war. Close by is Dinder House, a Georgian mansion, and to the north of the church is Wisteria House, with mullioned windows and built around 1700.

A New Stone Age axe, discovered in Dinder Wood can be seen in the museum at Wells.

Dinnington

Dinnington, south east of Ilminster and south west of Lopen on the great Roman road known as the Fosse Way and close to the site of a Roman villa, is thought to have belonged to Glastonbury Abbey in the 10th and 11th centuries. The village is clustered on rising ground and is characterised by sunken lanes.

A stream rising in the grounds of Hinton Park formerly drove a mill. There was a watermill in Dinnington in 1086, valued at 8d. In the 19th century a succession of pools were excavated to provide power for cheese and butter making.

Most local folk were employed on the nearby arable and dairying farms and also tended the orchards and manor gardens. Flax and potatoes were grown and they kept pigs and poultry. The women folk were kept busy with dressmaking, bonnet making and glove-making. Today farming remains the principal occupation.

Ditcheat

On the south east of the Pennard Ridge, about 6 miles to the south of Shepton Mallet lies the village of Ditcheat, a former manor of Glastonbury Abbey. In those days when a plough team consisted of 8 oxen, there was land enough there for 30 plough teams to work. This was an open field village, not fully enclosed until as recently as 1844.

The church reflects its Glastonbury connections in the richness of its fabric. An ancient mural of St Christopher, with a child on his shoulder and fish swimming at his feet, which lay forgotten for generations behind the plaster on the wall was brought to light earlier this century. A beautifully carved reading desk was fashioned from the pew of the Leir family, who provided rectors between 1699 and 1891. Richard Alleine, who was rector here for 50 years had two notable sons; Richard, who became rector of Batcombe in 1641 and much idolised by his flock, and William, a man of learning and of conscience who was rector of Blandford and much ill treated for his political opinions.

The 'Armless Wonder', William Kingston, was born in Ditcheat in

1765 without arms or shoulders. Remarkably, he overcame his disibilities to lead a full and active life. He married twice and fathered numerous normal children.

Doulting

The still active quarries of Doulting, on the southern fringe of the Mendips, just east of Shepton Mallet supplied oolite limestone for the building of Wells Cathedral and Glastonbury Abbey.

Doulting also has associations with the remarkably talented St Aldhelm, Saxon Bishop of Sherborne and Abbot of Malmesbury, who was an outstanding scholar, administrator and musician as well as having an attractive personality that people could relate to. It is said that he used to sing and entertain in the market place, and having gathered a following would gradually introduce a religious message to his audience.

St Aldhelm was taken ill in 709, while visiting his rich, pagan uncle, Kenred. Realising that he was about to die, and thinking it unappropriate to do so in a heathen house, he instructed his aides to carry him to the little wooden church, where he died on a stone slab. His spirit appeared later that day to his friend Bishop Eigwin of Worcester, instructing that his body be taken to Malmesbury for burial. The carrying out of this post-mortal wish became a 7 day pilgrimage across country, led by a priest carrying a cross followed by monks with lighted tapers, thus creating an imposing ecclesiastical pageant. Memorial crosses were erected at overnight stopping places along the route.

The present church, which occupies the site of that earlier wooden structure, is an Early English cruciform building with an octagonal tower and a spire, and a handsome south porch. An ancient churchyard cross is carved with symbols of the Passion.

The late 17th century Manor Farm has an impressive tithe barn, which was one of the many storehouses of the Abbey of Glastonbury.

Cranmore, to the east of Doulting is a Mecca for rail enthusiasts. The original East Somerset Railway opened in 1858, but the railway of today, officially opened in 1975 is run mostly by volunteers. There is an engine shed and workshops and a wide variety of attractions for visitors. Steam locomotives operate a service between Cranmore and Mendip Vale between April and October.

Dowlish Wake

Dowlish Wake, which lies alongside a brook in an area characterised by intersecting lanes evolved directly from the trackways linking old enclosures, now finds itself in the heart of a rural area bounded by the present day A303, A356, A30, A358 and A3037. The Crewkerne-Ilminster road, which ran through Kingstone and was turnpiked in 1759 ran about a mile to the north of the village where there was a gate and toll cottage. In an area of small villages, Dowlish Wake emerged as one of the biggest.

The church, the manor house and the 19th century Parke House lie to the north of the brook, while the medieval rectory, shops and a miscellany of old and modern houses are on its other side. There was a blacksmith's shop in the village, and appropriately, perhaps, the New Inn was formerly called The Horseshoe. Social life was always quite strong with a variety of organised activities. Facilities included a Friendly Society, Men's Club, Reading Rooms and a school now in use as the village hall, not to mention the services of a 'herbal doctoress' in the middle of the last century, fulfilling a role which is now finding its way back into fashion.

Agricultural and factory work was carried out by the men, and many women and girls produced cloth at home as a cottage industry. There had long been a tradition of milling in the area, for a water mill was granted to Monkton Farleigh priory at the start of the 13th century and corn mills, fulling mills and others harnessed the water power of the streams.

The church of St Andrew, constructed of Ham stone rubble and ashlar was much restored in 1861-62, but the chancel dates from the early 13th century, and contains the tomb of the explorer Captain John Hanning Speke (1827-1864). A member of a Somerset family born in Devonshire, he came to the Ilminster area when his father inherited estates in Somerset. Having served in the Indian army he became an African explorer, discovering Lake Tanganyika and the source of the Nile. Honours awaited him in England, but it is perhaps ironical that the explorer, having faced deadly perils in festering foreign climes should have met his death in a shotgun accident.

Cider has been produced here for centuries and is still fermented from local apples in the age old style. Today visitors can sample the range at Perry's Cider Mills before purchasing, and enjoy the associated collection of country bygones on display in the 16th century thatched barn.

Kingstone, just to the north, possesses some attractive cottages and a church with a central tower and fragments of 15th century glass. Cricket Malherbie, with its 19th century church and Cricket Court, built on the site of an Elizabethan manor house for Admiral Pitt around the same time, lies to the south west of Dowlish Wake.

Downhead, *see* Leigh-on-Mendip

Downside, *see* Stratton-on-the-Fosse

Draycott, *see* Rodney Stoke

Drayton, *see* Curry Rivel

Dulverton

Early routes converged on the little Exmoor market town of Dulverton, snugly situated amidst the hills on the banks of the River Barle in an area charmingly described by Tennyson as a 'land of bubbling streams.' The ageing poet stayed here with his son in 1891 at the Carnarvon Arms, just a year before his death. Still on a literary theme, the place was frequently referred to in R.D. Blackmore's novel *Lorna Doone* as being the home of John Ridd's Uncle Huckabuck.

In former times silver and lead were mined here. With its narrow streets, old bridge and fast flowing river it has an individual, moorland town charm, and has traditionally attracted attention as a hunting and angling centre. Its church of All Saints, possessing a 13th century tower was largely rebuilt in 1852, and an old sycamore tree in the churchyard pleasingly became known as The Belfry Tree. It once had a railway station, close to Brushford, where the church contains a chapel designed by Sir Edwin Lutyens, and an altar tomb to a man of many talents — diplomat, linguist, poet and traveller Colonel Aubrey Herbert, one time commander of an Albanian regiment, born at neighbouring Pixton Park. Sir George Williams, who founded the YMCA was born on a remote farm at Ashway, to the north west of Dulverton, and received his early education at a dame school in the town.

Dulverton is set amidst magnificent scenery, making it an ideal centre for walking, fishing, riding, touring or just enjoying the peace and tranquillity of the countryside, and it has a Tourist Information Centre.

Dunster

Between the wooded hills of Exmoor and the sea is well known Dunster, a place which has enchanted many a tourist. Strictly speaking Dunster is a town, a perfect feudal survival dominated by its splendid medieval castle standing on a knoll in the style of all the best story books. Dunster, formerly a centre for the woollen trade had become a market town by 1100, and a borough by 1197. By the 13th century it had gained prosperity from the wool trade as well as enjoying the advantages brought to the place by the Mohun and Luttrell families who occupied the fortified mansion. The River Avill, now silted up, was once wide and deep enough for Dunster to be a port. Today the famous Yarn Market still graces the wide, old world main street lined by attractive buildings, and the old packhorse bridge across the River Avill still leads the way to Gallox Hill, formerly known as Gallows Hill because two of Monmouth's followers were hanged here by Judge Jeffreys.

Dunster Castle was built on a natural hill by the Normans around the beginning of the 11th century and was in the possession of the Mohun family until 1404, when Joan, Lady Mohun was succeeded by Sir Hugh Luttrell. It remained in that family until it was made over to the National Trust in 1976. The present gatehouse was built in 1421 by Sir Hugh Luttrell. Many of the Luttrell family fought in the French wars, and Dunster was the scene of strife in the time of Stephen and in the Civil War, when it was besieged by Robert Blake. Standing in a 28 acre park, this fortified house was remodelled by Anthony Salvin in the 19th century. The house, grounds and park are now open to the public.

The magnificent church is reckoned to be the best of the West Country churches, and really comprises two churches, the Priory Church and the Parish Church. Until 1498 it was used by the parishioners and monks of the Benedictine Priory; after the Dissolution the historian Leland recorded that 'The hole chirch of the late Priory servith now for the paroche chirch'. The remains of the ancient Priory are to the north west of the church, with the monks' barn and dovecote nearby. The monks were the only people permitted to keep doves, which tended to raid the farmers' crops. Doves were reared for the monks' table. The Tithe Barn, now used as an estate workshop, has been largely rebuilt, but retains its 15th century door.

Dunster Castle Mill, on the River Avill beneath Castle Tor, an 18th century mill on the site of a mill mentioned in the Domesday Survey of 1086, was restored to working order in 1979. As a National Trust property it is now open to the public.

Wassailing the apple trees is customary in this part of Somerset between January 6th and 17th, and before they ventured out into the chilly orchards they performed the ceremony of Burning the Ashen Faggot whereby warming drinks were purchased every time the faggot exploded. Wassailing the apple tees is still carried out at nearby Carhampton (*see* Carhampton).

Dunster, the Yarn Market

On May Day the custom was for Hobby Horses with cows' tails to make their noisy way with plenty of fun and music through the streets. This reputedly stems from the day before May Day in 1772 when a dead cow was the only object to reach the shore from a sinking ship off Dunster. Its tail was cut off and used by toll collectors. Even less substantial is the ghostly white horse which occasionally rises up out of the middle of the road between here and Hinkley Point, and gallops a short distance before disappearing and re-appearing – causing motorists to take evasive action.

Durleigh

Durleigh Reservoir, 2 miles to the west of Bridgwater attracts wildfowl and is famous for its trout. On the edge of the reservoir is part of the formerly large manor house, now known as West Bower Farm. With its turrets, conical roofs and mullioned windows, it was described in one early guidebook as 'a very picturesque bit of masonry', and by Arthur Mee as 'a curious building with two round towers circled with grotesque gargoyles.' Once in the possession of the Seymour family, it is locally reputed to be the birthplace of Jane Seymour, 'the fairest, discreetest and most meritious of King Henry VIII's wives,' although Wulfhall in Wiltshire would dispute such a claim. The old, thatched dovecote contained 900 niches made of mud for the nesting birds.

The village church possesses a bell, reputed to be the oldest in the county.

Durston

Where the hills begin to fall away to the low moors to the north east of Taunton, lies the village of Durston. Traditionally on through routes, it is close to the old Bridgwater and Taunton Canal, the motorway and the junction of the Paddington to Penzance and Bristol lines. Back in 1853 the Bristol & Exeter opened its branch line from Durston via Athelney to Yeovil, and in 1906 part of it was rebuilt as a short cut to the west via Castle Cary. The route from Durston via Athelney, Langport and Martock to Yeovil has now been 'axed'.

Durston had the early distinction of possessing a Priory and Preceptory of Mynchin Buckland of the Order of St John of Jerusalem, the Order's only women's Priory in England. However, all traces of it have long since vanished.

East Brent

At the foot of Brent Knoll, East Brent is situated between the triangle created by the A38 and A370, and spreads westwards. In common with Brent Knoll and Lympsham it was on the western perimeter of the Glastonbury Abbey estates (*see* Brent Knoll). The church at East Brent, with its graceful stone spire visible as a landmark for miles around, reflects this monastic past. It has a splendid plaster ceiling dating from 1637 and beautifully carved bench ends depicting religious symbols, the arms of Glastonbury Abbey and the initials of Abbot Selwood who had a summer residence here.

It was Archdeacon Denison, rector for 61 years, who died in 1896 and was buried here, who started the lively village tradition of celebrating the harvest home as a special feature with feasting and processions.

East Coker

This mellow, attractive village constructed of Ham Hill stone, lying to the south of Yeovil, enjoys seafaring and literary connections, and was once renowned for the quality of its sailcloth. William Dampier, 'buccaneer, explorer, hydrographer', who circumnavigated the world three times, was the first to explore the north-west coast of Australia and had a strait and an archipelago named after him, was born here in the cottage known as Hymerford House in 1651. He was navigator aboard the ship that rescued Alexander Selkirk, the castaway on whom Daniel Defoe based Robinson Crusoe. Other sons of the parish to demonstrate wanderlust included Nicholas Dodge, founder of Block Island, and Andrew Elliott, baptised here in 1627 who also settled in America. The writer Thomas Stearns Eliot's Puritan ancestors emigrated from here to America, and T.S. Eliot's ashes were buried in the church at his particular wish. Like many descendants of those who emigrated to the 'new' countries, he had a yearning to discover his roots, and in his poem 'East Coker', written in 1940 he recorded his feelings thus:

'In my beginning is my end. Now the light falls
Across the open field, leaving the deep lane
Shuttered with branches, dark in the afternoon.
Where you lean against a bank while a van passes,
And the deep lane insists on the direction
Into the village . . .'

The village has some particularly attractive nooks and corners, including the drive beneath the trees with the church, Coker Court and the low, gabled Helyar almshouses, dating from around 1640. Coker Court, with a 15th century hall and early 17th century additions, formerly owned by the Courtenays, came into the possession of the Helyar family in 1616. The cosy, whitewashed village pub is appropriately named the Helyar Arms. Amongst the surrounding interesting farmhouses is Slades Farm, thought to date from the late 14th century.

Sutton Bingham, just to the south and close to the Dorset border possesses a little 12th century church with a beautiful chancel arch and mural paintings, a 17th century manor and a reservoir.

East Quantoxhead

The delightful unspoilt village of East Quantoxhead is approached down a steep, narrow, winding lane with the sea ahead and the Quantock Hills behind. Its thatched cottages, colourful gardens and millpond complete with ducks typify the perfect, much photographed English scene. The early historian Leland wrote: 'I saw a fair Park and Manor Place of the Lutterelles caullid Quantock Hedde bycause it standeth at the Heede of Quantock Hilles towards the Se.'

Court House stands on a bluff above the village and has been the home of the Luttrell family since the time of Domesday. The church, clinging to the hillside, attractive in its simplicity, has rough, grey walls and dark oak bench ends and pulpit.

The place is a delight for walkers with paths to the shore, Kilve Pill and Kilve Priory which can be a circular walk, or there are longer routes up into the hills which can also be done as a circuit. Quantoxhead is where the Quantock Hills meet the sea.

This village was the home of Sarah Biffin, born of humble parentage without arms, hands or legs and never growing beyond 37 inches tall. She was a lively and intelligent child, and despite such formidable handicaps she became an accomplished painter of miniatures, mastering the use of a pen, pencil and paintbrush by mouth. Incredibly, she also trained herself to use scissors and the needle. Originally receiving lessons from a Mr Dukes who took her around country fairs and circus side shows where she amazed audiences with her prowess, she was later befriended by the Earl of Morton who financed further training leading to the patronage of royalty and the award of a medal by the Society of Arts in 1827. Having thus become something of a celebrity, she was mentioned by Charles Dickens in *Nicholas Nickleby* and *Martin Chuzzlewit*. She was said to be good humoured with 'a round, merry face' and a 'lively, happy disposition.' Sadly, others reaped the greater part of financial rewards for her talents, and she died in impoverished circumstances in Liverpool on 2nd October 1850, at the age of 66.

Edington

On the Avalon side of the Poldens, Edington is one of the string of villages which had early connections with Glastonbury Abbey and were esteemed for their holy wells springing from the clays of the Lower Lias, containing water rich in medicinal salts. At the end of the 18th century Collinson wrote of Edington Well: 'A little below the church there is a perpetual spring, which contains sulphur and steel and stains silver yellow in two hours. Against the change of weather it smells like the foul barrel of a gun. It is very cold, leaves a white crust on the bodies it passes over and has been found efficacious in scorbutick (scurvy) cases.' Restored in memory of Margaret Charlotte Fownes Luttrell in 1937, it is located by the roadside. Some would claim that it is easy to detect by following one's nose, the 'Foul barrel of a gun smell' being sulphuretted hydrogen or 'bad egg gas', familiar to schoolchildren. The taste of the water fulfils the expectation of the pungent smell.

There is dissent amongst historians as to whether the Edington of the Poldens was the site of the battle of Ethandune, between the Saxons and the Danes, or Wiltshire's Edington was the true place. Following a decisive victory at Chippenham in Wiltshire, the Danes advanced on the Saxons, probably well aware that King Alfred had wintered on the marshes at Athelney. During the early part of 878,

Alfred carried out a number of sorties from the Somerset marshes. The advancing Danes were taken completely by surprise when they were finally attacked from the rear, resulting in the battle of Ethandune. Somerset would seem to have a strong case for Edington being the site, for it is close to Wedmore, where the peace was signed and also to Aller, where the Danish King Guthrum was subsequently baptised. It would be strange to relate this to Wiltshire.

Elworthy

The Brendon Hills, outliers of Exmoor, rise sharply to reach windswept summits of over 1,300 feet, from which there are spectacular views over wild countryside and across the Bristol Channel to Wales. There is a ten mile road along the partly wooded ridge from Wheddon Cross to Elworthy, which lies about 2 miles south of Monksilver, just off the B3188. Its small, low church has a 13th century tower, a delicately carved screen decorated with roses and thistles and rood loft stairs leading up to the old pulpit.

Elworthy Barrow, about 1½ miles to the south west of the village, is an unusually large earthwork which has been damaged by quarrying. In this desolate environment it is hardly surprising that imagination can run riot, and wild stories abound. An old woman living near Elworthy Barrow was suspected of being able to turn herself into a hare and lope about the hills, and some labourers, keen to put an end to her frolics decided to course her. Chased by their eager dogs, the hare showed amazing speed and promptly disappeared behind her cottage. When the men marched up to the door and thumped on it, a very breathless old lady opened it to see what all the fuss was about. Another version of the story is that they shot the hare in the leg, but it got away. However, it was seen as significant that the old lady walked with a limp thereafter.

Emborough

The tiny Mendip village of Emborough, with its well tended farms and bleak little church lies between Chewton Mendip and Gurney Slade. The natural Emborough Ponds in their delightful sylvan setting create a pleasing contrast to the rather forbidding Mendip landscape. The ponds, which can rapidly change their mood in accordance with the weather and the quality of the light, were described by Collinson in 1791 thus: 'At the bottom of a steep declivity is a fine lake called by the different names of Emberrow and Leachmore pond, containing nearly ten acres. It lies in a vale extending almost east and west with a beautiful plantation of firs, beeches and sycamores on the slopes of the hills on each side. On the eastern boundary is a small cottage and a boat house; at the west end is a marsh, and below that another lake much smaller.'

Enmore

Lying amongst the foothills of the Quantocks about 4 miles west of Bridgwater, is the charming village of Enmore with its ancient church dating from about 1185, its unique churchyard cross, the remains of a pseudo medieval castle built in 1779 and remodelled in Victorian times, rolling parkland and pleasing cottages.

The church contains many references to the Malet family, who were given the manor by William the Conqueror. This was acquired by John Perceval, Member of Parliament for Bridgwater who became the 2nd Earl of Egmont in the Irish peerage. This gentleman, who served as First Lord of the Admiralty and gave his name to Port Egmont in the Falklands was a clever scholar, genealogist and antiquarian, but regarded as humourless and eccentric. He had a particular bee in his bonnet about the medieval way of life, and nurtured a fantasy about the feudal system whereby he might be the all-powerful lord of the manor and others might acquiesce. Warming more and more towards this ideal, he tried to push a special Act through Parliament, and when that was thrown out he turned his attentions overseas — to the Isle of St John in the Gulf of St Lawrence. When this scheme proved abortive, he bought the Enmore estate. As part of his philosophy was that gunpowder would become obsolete and there would be a return to the medieval way of fighting, he took the precaution of constructing a castle with four massive corner towers, an inner courtyard, turreted gatehouse, and drawbridge over a dry moat which was operated by elaborate machinery. The place was described by a contemporary as: 'a singular structure, a large quadrilateral embattled pile of reddish, dark coloured stone, with semi-circular bastions at the corners and enclosing a spacious courtyard within.'

In 1833 much of this was demolished and the remains incorporated in the present house. During demolition work two helmets of the Malet family were discovered and these were removed to grace the walls of the church.

John Poole, cousin of Tom Poole, a friend of Coleridge and a host of eminent people, became rector of Enmore and founded one of the first elementary schools in 1810. Acclaimed as 'the cradle of free elementary education in this country,' it attracted great interest and he was 'visited from far and near by people of all ranks, and even foreigners.'

Exford

Routes from all over Exmoor converge at Exford, where a stone bridge replaces the original ford over the River Exe, which gave the place its name. It has associations with R.D. Blackmore's romantic novel *Lorna Doone*.

The church of St Mary Magdalene was formerly dedicated to the Celtic Saint Salvin. Traditionally there was boisterous jollification on the saint's feast day (22nd July), when the main pre-occupation was wrestling rather than saintly matters. In recent years sheep farming, tourism, fishing and hunting have been the mainstay of the village, and an annual horse show is held in August.

All around is evidence of prehistoric activity, and the heather clad Alderman's Barrow marked the boundaries of three parishes. Activity of a slightly different nature is reported on the road between Chetsford Bridge and Hawkcombe, where horses can suddenly become distressed and panic, and where eerie disembodied noises can sometimes be discerned.

Exton

To the south east of Exford, the village of Exton is perched picturesquely above the Exe Valley, where the River Quarme joins the River Exe to flow on southwards to the Devon border. The simple church of St Peter has herringbone masonry in the nave, of Norman origin.

Farleigh Hungerford

The village of Farleigh Hungerford is situated amidst beautiful scenery on the banks of the Frome, very close to the Wiltshire border, just east of Trowbridge. The name Farleigh is thought to have been derived from 'fair meadows'. The place was known to the Romans, for in the last century a Roman villa with fine tessellated floors was discovered here. From the reign of William Rufus until 1337, Farleigh was in the possession of the Montfort family, and when the ownership passed through other families and into the possession of the Hungerfords, the name was changed from Farleigh Montfort to Farleigh Hungerford. Sir Thomas Hungerford, first Speaker of the House of Commons forged ahead with rebuilding the manor house in substantial fortified style, only obtaining permission to do so when it had become a *fait accompli.* The Hungerfords served under Henry V at Agincourt, and occupied prestigious positions in the reign of Henry VI, married prudently, acquired more and more power, wealth and land, performed stirring deeds and at various times paid the price for doing so by losing their heads.

The first Lord Hungerford, the son of Sir Thomas, set about improving and expanding the estate and decided to claim the church as the family's private chapel. As this left the village folk without a church, a new one was built in the 15th century.

During the reign of Henry VIII the wife of Lord Walter Hungerford was imprisoned by him in one of the sturdy towers, and she suspected Lord Walter of trying to poison her. When he was beheaded for high treason, she married Sir Robert Throgmorton. At the time of Lord Walter Hungerford's execution alongside Thomas Cromwell in 1540, the castle was described as 'portly and very strongly buylded, havyng inward and outward wardes, and in the inward wardes many fayre chambers, a fayre large hall, on the hedde of which hall iij or iiij goodly greate chambers, with fayre and strong roffes, and dyvers other fayre lodginges, with all manner howses of offices.' By the end of the 18th century, when the family had died out, it had become a 'melancholy picture of fallen greatness.'

Today the castle has become a romantic ruin, and the chapel now serves as a museum with impressive family monuments and effigies, medieval armour and Lady Joan's will instructing that 12 torches carried by 12 poor women clothed in lowly russet should light the way to her funeral. She also left money to ensure that prayers be said for evermore for herself and her ancestors.

Tellisford, just to the south is a pretty, quiet place with a three arched bridge over the River Frome, which along this stretch divides Somerset from Wiltshire.

Fiddington

Between the Quantocks and Bridgwater Bay lies the delightful village of Fiddington with its 14th century church possessing a Jacobean pulpit, medieval bell and the remains of an ancient cross.

Fiddington lives up to the story-book charm of its name, for the place has long attracted tales of romantic and eerie goings on. Naturally there has to be a witch in a place called Fiddington, and even in this century folk have claimed to see her flying past on her broomstick. In days of yore there was a cautionary tale about a boastful blacksmith who was imprudent enough to proclaim that his skill was such that he could shoe the horse of the very Devil — to perfection. It just so happened that a traveller arrived on the stroke of midnight complaining that his horse had cast a shoe, and looking up into the rider's face the blacksmith realised that it was the Devil himself who had come to test him. Making an excuse that he had left his hammer at home, the terrified man rushed to the parson for help. The parson told him that he must carry out the work he had promised, and feeling, no doubt, that discretion is the better part of valour, escorted him part of the way back and waited by the hedge. The blacksmith set to work, and despite his quivering hands shoed the horse to perfection — just as he had claimed he could. But when it came to accepting the proffered sack of gold, he shook his head and explained that he never accepted payment for work carried out at night. The puzzled Devil glanced over his shoulder, and catching sight of the parson lurking behind the hedge screamed that he would have enticed the boastful blacksmith if it had not been for the interfering parson, 'vor zerten zure!' whereupon he and his evil steed disappeared in a flash of flame.

Two wealthy sisters, regarded as recluses, lived in a lonely cottage in the fields with a hired manservant. Occasionally they went away to take the waters at Bath, leaving their manservant in charge, but one absence was particularly noticed because neither the manservant nor his dog seemed to be around. The place became neglected and there were reports of flashing lights, eerie screams in the night and strange happenings in the area around the cottage. Eventually a search revealed two skeletons and an ominous looking knife. There were reports of a ghost on the footbridge nearby, supposedly that of the murderer, and local folk give the place a wide berth. Anyone pouring scorn on such nonsense and attempting to move into the cottage is said to move elsewhere rather quickly.

Fivehead

One of the finest viewpoints from which to savour the beauty of the Somerset Levels is Fivehead Hill. The village of Fivehead is situated on the Curry Rivel ridge and slopes down towards the low moors.

The striking beauty of the mauve and purple flowering heads of the unusual Teazle crop was once a characteristic sight around Fivehead and nearby villages, for the natural brushing qualities of its bristles were recognised by the West of England cloth industry for the scoring of newly woven cloth. Colloquially known as 'Fuller's Thistle', the Teazle, which is not a member of the thistle family, is a crop which takes 2 years to yield. Sown in April, it is earthed up in the summer, thinned in November, and the heads are cut the following year. The heads, now graded into 2 sizes were formerly graded into *Kings, Middlings* and *Scrubs,* and they were skilfully and decoratively packed in a style known as *'Staffing the Teazels.'* Unfortunately this art form has now disappeared. Today, Teazels are grown on a lesser scale, but the agricultural emphasis is on mixed farming here and in the other 'Teazle' villages.

Another custom, carried out at 21 yearly intervals is that of 'bidding by candle', whereby an inch of candle is lighted while land is auctioned. The property goes to the highest bidder at the time of the candle going out. Proceeds went to the upkeep of the church.

Galhampton

The A371, A303 and A359 encompass a triangle of hills and woodlands, dissected by streams, with a maze of lanes linking farms and small villages; Galhampton being near the top of the triangle, about 2 miles to the south of Castle Cary. There is an 18th century manor house, some pretty cottages, and an inn, formerly the New Inn, but now renamed 'The Harvester' with a modern signboard depicting a 'combine.' Almost opposite the inn is a handsome farmhouse with dripstones and a pillared porch constructed of the mellow, pleasing

Ham stone.

Nearby are the renovated Abbey Cottages containing remnants of medieval ecclesiastical building, and subsequent styles of architecture.

Goathurst

Set below a projecting spur of the Quantocks in an area of wooded hills and valleys where streams ripple over stones and tumble in pleasing cascades, the delightful village of Goathurst emerges as a place of much character and charm. From the slopes one can savour the prospect of the enchanting countryside and sea.

The 14th century red sandstone church, dedicated to St Edward the Martyr, contains many impressive monuments to the Tynte family, who derived their unusual name from a young knight who so distinguished himself during the Crusades at the Battle of Ascalon in 1192, when dressed all in white and mounted on a white charger he bore himself as bravely as a lion, and performed heroic deeds equal to those of six crusaders. This shining example of masculinity, on which subsequent generations of ladies have based their ideal of Manhood — in vain, was publicly praised by Richard the Lionheart, who conferred on him the Arms of a Lion Argent on a 'Field Gules between Six Crosslets of the first,' and the Motto *'Tynctus cruore Saraceno'*.

Halswell House, built by Sir Halswell Tynte in 1689 in 'as beautiful a situation as may be found anywhere in Somerset' on the site of an earlier structure, was described by Nikolaus Pevsner as 'the most important house of its date in the county'. The park was adorned with romantic and whimsical follies and grottoes, which included the Rotunda with Ionic portico, a Druid's Temple and Robin Hood's Temple. Some of the remaining splendour of a bygone age can be recalled by older village folk. In recent times the place has been taken over for residential purposes.

Godney

Associated with the Avalon of Arthurian legend, Godney, to the north west of Glastonbury, was one of the lake villages which flourished from around 250 BC . Godney and other places with names ending in 'ey', 'y' or 'oy' indicated a settlement on an island, for in earlier times a vast section of Somerset was under water or swampy, and the mounds projecting above the surface were referred to as islands.

The lake villages, with high protective fences or pallisades, were constructed on mounds of clay with a base of timber and brushwood. The causeways were also protective, gave access and acted as landing stages for their craft. The buildings, which in later times were circular, were constructed of wattle and daub and had thatched roofs. The lake village dwellers were highly skilled craftsmen who had great appreciation of beautiful and functional things, and led organised, communal lives. There is very little to be seen on site today, but the many remarkable finds on display in museums in Glastonbury and Taunton give us a fascinating insight into their way of life (*see* Meare).

Godney, together with other lands was granted to the monks by Cenwealh, King of the West Saxons towards the end of his reign in the 7th century. The handsome 19th century church was constructed in the Norman style in an area of reclaimed marshland.

Gupworthy

Gaping shafts, slag heaps, old railtracks, ruined engine houses, cottages and chapels now overgrown and almost absorbed into the landscape tell a story of brief but intense 19th century industrial activity hereabouts. In fact there had been earlier exploitation of the iron ore of the Brendons in the 16th century, when German engineers were invited here to provide technical advice.

By the early 1840s the area around Luxborough was being mined, and in 1853, when the Brendon Hills Iron Ore Company was founded the West Somerset Mineral Line was extended to Gupworthy, then terminated at Goosemoor. The line descended a spectacular 800 feet at a 1 in 4 gradient known as the Comberow Incline to the Washford valley and then to the port of Watchet. Wagons were raised and lowered by cables and powered by steam. There was tremendous pride in the venture, and there were great celebrations when the line was officially opened to passengers between Watchet and Comberow (pronounced 'Combe Row') and it continued to be a well supported service. Passengers were allowed to ride up the incline free but at their own risk. However, the main function of the railway was to transport the ore to Watchet, from where it was shipped to Newport in Wales. The ore from these workings fed the smelting furnaces of Ebbw Vale, and were particularly suitable for the making of Bessemer steel.

For the miners, life was harsh, the wages low and prospects bleak; Good Friday and Christmas Day were the only two holidays of the year. But miners and their families were traditionally long suffering. There was a highly developed sense of community and they enjoyed rallies, sports, tea parties and other get togethers, where the accent was firmly on temperance. When the mines closed, 'distress funds' were set up to help these mining folk. Today this area has taken on immense significance for those interested in industrial archaeology.

Gurney Slade

The hamlet of Gurney Slade straddles a rather dusty main road in an area of the Mendips which has been mined for coal and lead and quarried for its limestone, and has something of the air of the Welsh mining valleys. In the 17th century there was considerable lead mining activity around Gurney Slade and Binegar with the iron ore being carted to smelting works in the valleys. This died out over a century ago. Licences to mine had to be obtained from the 'Lord Royal', and miners staked their claims in traditional style and started digging their 'grooves' or 'gruffs'. Today hummocky, excavated ground on the Mendip plateau is still referred to as 'gruffy' ground (*see* Charterhouse).

There was a time when local workers spent the summer months quarrying and worked in the nearby brewery at Oakhill in the winter. In these days of mechanisation fewer are employed in the quarries. The neighbouring village of Binegar was well known locally for its annual Whitsuntide horse fair.

The prehistoric Blacker's Hill camp, above the valley of Gurney Slade was described in an old guidebook as 'a sequestered romantic dell, watered by a rivulet which works an ancient mill.'

Haddon Hill, *see* Upton

Halse, *see* Ash Priors

Hardington Mandeville

This lovely village with the stylish, melodic ring to its double-barrelled name is situated to the south west of Yeovil along Somerset's southern border with Dorset, where it is common to have places with two part names. The area has an elevated feel about it and is characterised by hills and ridges and commanding views across some outstandingly beautiful countryside. Nearby is Hamdon Hill, capped by an Iron Age fort confusingly known as Ham Hill which is famous for its mellow toned golden limestone from which Hardington Mandeville and the surrounding towns and villages were built, and which adds warmth and charm to the pleasing local architecture.

The low towered church of St Mary the Virgin dates from Norman times, and in 1863 renovation work designed by Rev John Hancock, a former rector was carried out in Neo-Norman style. Today the area remains mainly agricultural, and people living here and in neighbouring villages work in Yeovil or Crewkerne.

To the south east lies the little village of Pendomer with its little church containing momentoes to the Domare or Dummer family, and ancient manor house, now in use as a farm.

Haselbury Plucknett

The historian Leland wrote of Haselbury Plucknett, north east of Crewkerne and close to the Dorset border, 'at this place lyvid the Holy Hermite and Prophete Wulfrik in King Henry I Dayes'. Born at Compton Martin in the Mendips, this one time sport loving country squire cast aside his hawk and hounds to become a priest, having learnt spiritual values from a beggar. He retreated into a hermit's cell near the church of Haselbury Plucknett, and devoted his life to prayer and physical deprivation. It was his custom to take a daily cold bath and remain in it until he had recited the entire Book of Psalms, and to dress in chain mail, conveniently shortened to a suitable length for kneeling and unhindered praying. He was widely famed as counsellor, miracle worker and prophet, receiving such visitors as St Bernard and King Henry I and Stephen. He actually foretold Stephen's rise to the throne when his uncle was King. He seemed capable of achieving miracles by the power of thought, for during King Henry's visit an attendant named Drogo, inclined to mock, was effectively put in his place by suddenly becoming paralysed. Wulfric's strange powers left people dumbfounded, but on one occasion the effect was just the reverse of that, for a man dumb from birth was miraculously given the ability to speak not only in English, but in Latin as well. It is said that the saint saved poor wretches from the Devil.

When the celebrated saint and hermit died at the ripe old age of 90 in 1154, the monks of Montacute tried to claim his body after it had been buried in his cell by the Bishop of Wells. However, his remains were closely guarded and re-interred inside the church.

Today the church is much restored, and Haselbury Plucknett, another south Somerset village with a double barrelled name, emerges as a very attractive place with handsome buildings constructed of the local Ham Hill stone. Within the churchyard of St Michael and All Angels are nesting boxes and a specially designated Nature Conservation Area; a forward-looking trend well worth emulating.

Hatch Beauchamp

This village, situated about 5 miles to the south east of Taunton just off the A358, derived its pleasing name from the powerful Beauchamp family who arrived in Somerset at the time of the Norman Conquest and acquired extensive lands.

Hatch Beauchamp, on the western side of the 'finely waved and indented' slopes of the Curry Rivel ridge extending almost to Langport was close to the course of the now disused branchline from Taunton to Chard Junction and to the course of the old Chard canal.

Hatch Court, bearing the date 1775, is a fine Palladian style house constructed of Bath stone. Its mainly 15th century church of St John the Baptist, set in picturesque parkland has a parapet, pinnacles, fine belfry windows, a 16th century font and bench ends depicting fighting cocks, St John the Baptist and St George and the dragon. The place has a number of proud and patriotic associations. One of its windows honours Colonel J.R.M. Chard V.C., R.E., hero of Rorke's Drift, who died at his brother's rectory at Hatch in 1897, and is buried in the churchyard here. As Lieutenant Chard he was in command of Rorke's Drift when it was attacked by 3,000 Zulus on 22nd January 1879. At the time the garrison was made up of 8 officers and 131 N.C.O's and men, 35 of whom were patients at the base's small hospital. Although heavily outnumbered, they defended the base until relief came, thus saving Natal from a large Zulu invasion. Queen Victoria sent a wreath to Colonel Chard's funeral, which occupied a place beneath his memorial window for some years. The Royal Engineers come to pay regular homage here.

The four corner carvings of dogs on the church tower may have associations with the hounds traditionally used for trailing and hunting in Neroche forest. Carvings such as these, colloquially known around these parts as 'hunky punks', were functional and broke the straight lines of dull sections of masonry. The intriguing term 'hunky punk' is thought to have been derived from the Old English 'hunkers', which described squatting on the haunches and 'punchy', indicating a short, squat appearance.

Nearby Wrantage, just north of Crimson Hill on the A378 between Langport and Taunton bears the remains of the old Taunton Canal, which failed as a result of the coming of the railway — a fact which may give travellers caught up in traffic hold ups amidst exhaust fumes pause for reflection.

Hawkridge

The intriguing little hamlet of Hawkridge, with its church and handful of buildings, is perched high on a ridge above the River Barle to the north west of Dulverton. In its elevated and beautiful setting well away from main roads and life's hurly burly, it has an aura of tranquillity increasingly difficult to find these days. In winter-time particularly, it must be one of Exmoor's loneliest places.

In medieval times the habitation was referred to as Haweckrig, which means *Hawks' ridge*, a place that any self-respecting hawk would be pleased to colonize. Along the river to the south east are the remains of the twin fortesses which guarded this valley, Brewer's Castle and Mounsey Castle, but now overgrown earthworks.

Just to the north and about 1,000 feet below lies the famous old clapper bridge of Tarr Steps. Very cleverly constructed to stand the test of time, it has taken a battering on various occasions; in more recent times in the floods of 1947 and 1952. A guidebook written earlier this century stated, 'Nothing can be lovelier than the valley at Tarr Steps', and hordes of modern day visitors would re-echo that sentiment. The precise date and origin of the bridge are unknown, but in Somerset there is always a tale to explain everything. It seems that the cunning old Devil himself built the bridge in one night to get him across the river, and being an awkward kind of a chap, he didn't want anyone else to make use of his bridge. An incautious cat who tried to venture across did not live to recount the tale. However, a rector of Hawkridge did not think he or his flock should put up with this sort of nonsense, so he ventured down to the bridge, and when the Devil shouted insults at him, he hurled even worse insults back. Exactly what was said has been lost in the mists of mythology, but apparently the good rector won the slanging match, and thereby also the right of folk to use the bridge.

Another vigorous tradition concerned the Monday before Shrove Tuesday, when villagers enjoyed the custom of the throwing of the Old Cloam (pottery). As the earthenware thudded against cottage doors revellers would chant:

'Tippetty, tippetty tin,
Give me a pancake and I will come in.
Tippetty, Tippetty toe,
Give me a pancake
And I will go!'

If the cheeky youngsters were caught in the ensuing scuffle, their faces would be blackened before they were given their reward of pancakes.

Heddon Oak, *see* Stogumber

Henstridge

Close to Somerset's zigzagging south eastern borders with north Dorset, and between Sherborne and Shaftesbury, is the village of Henstridge, situated near the junctions of the A30 and A357. This was the 'Mellstock Cross' with the 'white handpost' of Thomas Hardy's 'By Henstridge Cross At The Year's End', but today traffic lights have replaced that white handpost. Henstridge was also on the route of the much loved Somerset and Dorset railway.

Nearby Sherborne Castle was leased by Sir Walter Raleigh from Queen Elizabeth, and the Virginia Ash Inn, now the Virginia Ash Hotel near the crossroads, has the distinction — or notoriety — of being the place where Sir Walter lit up his first tobacco pipe, much to the astonishment of local folk. The story goes that the serving-man fearing that he had set himself on fire rushed for a bucket of water and doused him down. A number of other places claim this rather unlikely happening.

The church, largely rebuilt during the last century retains some 15th century work. Of particular interest is a fine, canopied altar tomb with effigies of Sir William Carent, high sheriff of Somerset and Dorset clad in armour, and his wife in a robe decorated with rosettes.

Around these borderlands at Christmastide there was a custom of pulling all the berries off the mistletoe — without being observed, for those caught in the act might find themselves chased — and given a kiss for each discarded berry. Some say there were some sharp eyes and slow runners around these parts come Yuletide!

Hestercombe House, *see* Kingston St Mary

Higher Wambrook, *see* Wambrook

High Ham

High Ham Hill was an island before the Somerset marshes were drained between the 10th and 14th centuries. Today this promontory, an outpost of the underlying rocks, rears up out of the levels in dramatic style, reaching a height of 280 feet above sea level. Thus it presents a delightful vantage point from which to savour views across the peat moors.

The village of High Ham which crowns the hill is quiet and picturesque, with delightful cottages, tall trees and a small village green. The church rebuilt in the 15th century by Abbot Selwood of Glastonbury has a fine 500 year old rood screen, a richly carved roof and some expressive and amusing gargoyles. Adrian Schael, rector of High Ham from 1570-1599, compiled a description of the parish in Latin.

Half a mile to the east of the village is a thatched windmill dating from 1822, and in use until 1910. Now in the care of the National Trust, it can be viewed by appointment. From medieval times numerous windmills dotted along the ridge between Aller and Somerton must have been a most pleasing work-a-day sight. Turn Hill, ½ mile to the north west and also owned by the National Trust, commands beautiful views across Sedgemoor to the coast.

High Ham Mill

Higher Chillington, *see* Chillington

Hillfarrance

In the Vale of Taunton, to the north east of Wellington, close to the meeting of Hillfarrance Brook and the River Tone lies the pleasant and peaceful village of Hillfarrance, sometimes known as Hill

Farrance, with its small green and fine church, which has a delicate parapet, 16th century tower, 17th century pulpit and beautifully crafted bench-ends.

In an area characterised by unspoilt countryside and numerous small farms, high speed trains skirt the village and roar their way westwards, while the disused branch line to the north and nearby sections of abandoned canal bear witness to quickly changing communications and technology. Back in the old days it was customary on Midsummer Eve for farming folk to lay a posy of flowers on the biggest stone they could find on the farm, for this was thought to bring them good luck.

Hinton St George

This stylish village, constructed mainly of the mellow tone Ham Hill stone, has handsome buildings, a wide main street and a medieval cross with a carving representing John the Baptist, capped with an 18th century ball finial.

The fates and fortunes of the place have been synonymous with those of the Poulett family, whose ancestral home for 500 years was Hinton House. Amias Poulett, probably the first of the family to have been born in the village, set about building the house after receiving a knighthood around 1490. Country squire and gentleman, he later became a soldier and Sheriff of Somerset and Dorset. It was during his time as Sheriff that he arrested the future Cardinal Wolsey for being drunk and disorderly at Lopen Fair and had him placed in the village stocks (*see* Lopen). One of the Poulett sons was christened Anne, a curious choice, whilst Susan, the daugher of the first Earl occasionally returns in ghostly form to rustle her skirts on the stairway.

Over the centuries the family was held in great esteem by the villagers who looked towards the Lord of the Manor for their livelihood, protection and guidance, and for their part the Pouletts devoted themselves to service, duty, responsibility and allegiance to King and Country. They were staunch Royalists, and probably as a result of this the village got very much caught up in the events of the Civil War, with troops quartered around the place, Hinton House standing out unsuccessfully against the Parliamentarians.

The villagers worked extremely hard for their first family, but also basked in their reflected prestige. Provisions were made educationally and medically for local folk, and the village school continues to function. In the past, 'upmarket' trades such as dressmaker, tailor, milliner, stationer, bookseller and land surveyor all flourished. In 1840 it was described as having a 'pleasing air of comfort and respectability.'

The charter of Hinton Fair was granted to the Lord of the Manor in 1633 to take place every year on St George's Day; sheep and cattle were sold in the market and brightly coloured stalls displayed their wares around the old market cross and along the streets.

Hinton St George, the medieval cross

'Punkie Night' traditions are thought to originate from a time when anxious wives went searching for errant husbands (who lingered too long at Chiselborough Fair) with 'punkies', which were lighted candles inside hollowed out turnips or mangold wurzels. On

Halloween Night village children still go around the village re-echoing the age old chant:

'Punkie Night,
Punkie Night,
It's Punkie Night tonight!
Adam and Eve
Wouldn't believe
It's Punkie Night tonight!'

That is repeated twice and when the door is opened they continue:

'Give us a candle,
Give us a light,
It's Punkie Night tonight!'

Hinton House was requisitioned during both wars, becoming a military hospital in the First World War and housing two schools in the Second World War. American troops from the nearby transit camp enjoyed dances at the Victory Hut, which has since been demolished, and joined in with village life, introducing the young folk to such luxuries as chewing gum, doughnuts, candies and coffee with cream.

Hinton St George was the birthplace in 1563 of Henry Cuff, Regius Professor of Greek at Oxford, who became secretary to the Earl of Essex and was executed for treason; it was also where Henry Fowler (1858-1933) lived while compiling the Oxford English Dictionary.

Holcombe

The former colliery village of Holcombe in the Mendips to the north east of Shepton Mallet is in an area rich in prehistory. The Fosse Way passes just over a mile to the west, the remains of a Roman villa was found nearby, while up on the hill is a long barrow, originally measuring 115 by 60 feet, and generally known as the Giant's Grave. A stream which rises in these hills and hurries its way along the intriguingly named Snail's Bottom flows on past Radstock to join Wellow Brook and the Avon. In earlier times, when the village was a hive of mining activity the fine quality local waters were ideal to use in the brewing of local beer, serving the needs of the workers.

Although the village has a church built in 1884, the former parish church of St Andrew, pleasingly set in the countryside in splendid isolation a mile to the north of the village is the one which captures everyone's imagination. Impressive in its artless simplicity, this little church has associations with Scott of the Antarctic, whose father, mother, brother and sister are buried in the churchyard. An added inscription states: 'And in memory of Robert Falcon Scott, C.V.O. Captain, R.N., who in returning from the South Pole with his companions was translated by a glorious death, March, 1912'.

Holford

Somerset enjoyed rather brief, but close associations with the poets Sir Henry Newbolt, Samuel Taylor Coleridge, William Southey and William Wordsworth. Wordsworth was living close to the Dorset border south of Crewkerne with his sister Dorothy when he first met the younger Coleridge, then residing at Nether Stowey, and having struck up a warm and stimulating friendship they moved to Alfoxton House, just outside Holford to be near to him. They found inspiration in the varied and colourful landscape of the Quantocks and it was as they walked these hills that Coleridge discussed with Wordsworth the idea for the poem *The Ancient Mariner* that was beginning to take shape in his mind.

They jointly produced *Lyrical Ballads* in 1798 which began with *The Ancient Mariner* and included some of Wordsworth's finest verse, although it was some considerable time before this work was recognised for its value in the literary world. Dorothy Wordsworth, similarly inspired by these literary walks through the Somerset landscape recorded in her Alfoxton Journal: 'There is everything here; sea, woods wild as fancy ever painted, brooks, clear and pebbly as in Cumberland, villages so romantic . . .' and went on to reveal that 'Our principal inducement was Coleridge's society'. They similarly enjoyed visits from Charles Lamb, Hazlitt and others of the literary set. However, their apparently strange goings on with nocturnal walks taking stools, telescopes, notebooks and other equipment, together with the Wordsworths' alien north country accent and Dorothy's swarthy complexion, aroused suspicion and mistrust among the local folk, with the result that they were suspected of spying for the French. To Coleridge, Alfoxton dell was 'rather a place to make men forget there is any necessity for treason,' but the suspicions caused the poets to exchange the delights of Somerset for Germany. Wordsworth wrote of that idyllic summer:

'That Summer, under whose indulgent skies,
Upon smooth Quantock's airy ridge we roved
Unchecked, or loitered mid her sylvan combes,
Thou, in bewitching words with happy heart,
Didst chaunt the vision of that Ancient Man,
The bright eyed Mariner, and rueful woes
Didst utter of the Lady Cristabel.'

Today Alfoxton House is a hotel, but its position is as beautiful and commanding as ever.

In the village of Holford, pretty cottages mingle with pleasant houses. The small church with its gabled tower was largely rebuilt in the 19th century, but the shaft of an old cross remains. A very unusual historical feature to survive is a dog pound which remains in a remarkably good state of preservation. The ancient Plough Inn is reputed to be haunted by a 'Spanish traveller', who had accumulated wealth and was murdered in his bedchamber there in 1555.

The land to the south and west of Holford is characterised by tracts of gorse and bracken, beautiful Quantock beeches and steeply sided, wooded combes with plantations of oak and conifers and sparkling, clear water cascading from the summits. There is a delightful little tarn at the head of Holford Glen. The Quantock Hills, with their network of ancient trackways, forts, barrows, tumuli, cairns and the remains of ancient settlements bear witness to intense prehistoric activity. Today much of this area is in the care of the National Trust.

Holman Clavel

Tucked away in the beautiful, unspoilt Blackdown Hills, about 7 miles to the south of Taunton, and close to the Somerset and Devon border is Holman Clavel, also known at various times as 'Holmin' and 'Holmen'. Situated where 6 lanes converge in symmetrical style, and in a landscape rich in prehistory, the indications are that the place was once much more important.

There are various theories as to the origin of the name, which could incorporate those of previous landowners, as was traditional. However, it is popularly thought to reflect the local dialect words for holly and the lintel beams over the old open fireplaces. Possibly warming to this theme, the Holman Clavel Inn, situated in isolation at the meeting of the ways, is reputed to have a friendly hearthside sprite, affectionately known as 'Chimney Charlie', who tends to assert himself when folk scoff or question his existence!

The symbolic theme of holly is deeprooted in the traditions of the Blackdowns, for around these parts there were variations on *The Carol of the Holly Boy and the Ivy Girl*, incorporting the refrain 'O, the ivy O, she'd grow, she'd grow' and adapting each of the four verses to suit each season, concluding that:

'O, the ivy, O, she's queen of old
And the holly, he is red,
Hang'n high on the farm,
Us won't come to harm,
'Till the Chrissimass Days be told
O, 'tis ivy O, green ivy, O,
O, the ivy, O, she's Queen of old.'

Holywell Lake, *see* **Sampford Arundel**

Horner, *see* **Luccombe**

Huish Champflower

Set beside the River Tone at the edge of the Brendon Hills and to the south of Clatworthy Reservoir, the village, which has a gentle, poetic ring to its name, possesses some delightful cottages and a church dating mainly from the 15th century.

Around these parts it was considered unlucky to praise a new born baby to its face — so step behind the cradle before admiring his dimples.

Huish Episcopi

To the east of Langport, and almost absorbed by the town, is the proudly named Huish Episcopi, with its magnificent church constructed of Blue Lias with Ham stone dressings in a delightful, leafy setting. The stone tracery of the tower is acknowledged to be among the finest in Somerset. This handsome church was featured on a postage stamp in 1972.

Huntspill

To the south of Burnham-on-Sea lies the strung out village of Huntspill, dominated by its massive 15th century church tower, silhouetted against the wide expanse of sky, and buttressed against coastal storms in this exposed situation. The village is said to derive its name from Hun (or Hune), a local hero who led his troops to victory in the Battle of Ellandune against Beornwulf, King of Mercia, and who died in his hour of triumph.

The land hereabouts once belonged to the Dean and Chapter of Wells Cathedral, which had responsibility for the upkeep of the seawalls, protecting large areas of reclaimed land. Sixty years after the removal of this monastic control, the seawall gave way, resulting in extensive flooding, whereby 30 villages were submerged and many people were drowned, including 28 inhabitants of Huntspill.

In the 1770's another major reclamation scheme was underway, with the construction of a seawall allowing tidal mudflats to stabilise as meadowland. However, this was unpopular with local folk who had enjoyed ancient common rights on the moor. The landscape became totally transformed, but the problems of flooding were not solved until the beginning of the Second World War when a channel was dug, thus creating the Huntspill River as we know it today. As well as improving the drainage of the Somerset Levels, it provided essential water to an ordnance factory at Puriton.

A gazeteer of 1909 accompanies the traveller southwards, before the existence of the Huntspill River, thus: 'The road, worn into saucer shaped holes by excess of motor traffic, goes straight and flat across the Level, with pollard willows and stagnant, duckweedy ditches on either side, and so through the wayside hamlet of West Huntspill; a naturally slovenly, out-at-elbow place, not improved by being nowadays thickly coated with motor dust'. Which all goes to show that everything is relative!

Hurcott, *see* Seavington St Mary

Ilton

Two miles to the northwest of Ilminster, and close to the now disused railway branchline and canal, Ilton derives its name from being along the course of the River Isle. Its church bears many memorials to the Wadham family, which had an apparent preference for the name of Nicholas; a state of affairs which can cause confusion for historians.

Sir Nicholas Wadham (1561-1609) who with his wife Dorothy founded Wadham College, Oxford, lived at the manor house of Merrifield, which formerly stood a mile to the west of the village and was surrounded by a moat. The moat is still there, but nothing remains of the house. It was recorded that this 'hospitable house was an inn at all times, a court at Christmas'.

To the south west of the church are the attractive almshouses with quaint, thatched dormers, mullioned windows and projecting chimney breasts which were founded by Nicholas Wadham in the 17th century. Along the Stocklinch road are further almshouses, with pleasing, mullioned windows, founded in 1634 by 'John Whetstone, Gentleman'. His is a reputedly rags-to-riches story, for having been discovered in a manger with a bundle of whetstones as a new-born baby, he acquired that name, and was cared for by villagers. Determined to justify his existence, he adopted a positive approach to life and became successful and wealthy. But he never forgot his early life and those who helped him. The cottages were founded as a way of helping village folk in need, as he had been helped.

Rushes were traditionally harvested around the area in the autumn, which, in earlier times was an occasion for celebration, with processions and the carrying of rush brooms.

Isle Abbots (or Ile Abbots)

Somerset's fine church towers are seen to best effect when they dominate the flatlands and are seen in relief against a wide skyscape in all its varying moods. The church at Isle Abbots, which does just that, is considered to be a first rate example of demonstrating the lyrical expression of the local craftsmen's genius. This church of the Taunton Deane type has a notable tower with double windows in the belfry stage, rather than in the stage below. It has pinnacled buttresses, and niches with statues fashioned with exquisite detail.

Isle Abbots

The place derives its name from its position on the River Isle which is a tributary of the Parrett, and its connection with abbots stems from the time when the land was chartered to abbeys and churches by the Wessex kings in the 7th century.

Isle Abbots is in the heart of an area where teazels were traditionally grown for the cloth industry to raise the nap on tweedy materials. Teazels are still grown today in this mixed farming region (*see* Fivehead).

Isle Brewers (or Ile Brewers)

In teazel growing country to the east of Isle Abbots is Isle Brewers, deriving its name from its position on the River Isle and from being the early estate of the De Bruyere, Briwere or Brewer family. Lord William Brewer was a remarkable man who achieved much for the area by co-operating with Kings Henry II, Richard I, John and Henry III. He obtained from King John a charter for Bridgwater in 1200 as well as forging ahead with plans to construct a castle and found an Augustinian Hospital of St John there.

The unusual church with its red roof and red capped tower was rebuilt in 1861 by the eccentric Dr Joseph Wolff, son of a Jewish rabbi, born in Bavaria in 1795, who having turned Christian set about preaching to Jews in Jerusalem. He travelled extensively in the East as a nomadic missionary and experienced the sort of adventures that a writer of fiction would find difficulty in dreaming up, such as searching for lost tribes, being shipwrecked, becoming enslaved, travelling for hundreds of miles having been robbed of his clothes and his money, contracting cholera in Spain and recovering to journey on to Abyssina and the U.S.A. and miraculously escaping execution in Bokhara. His was not the meek and mild approach to Christianity, for he signed himself 'Apostle of Our Lord Jesus Christ for Palestine, Persia, Bokhara and Balkh'.

Keinton Mandeville

To the north of Yeovil and close to the Fosse Way, Keinton Mandeville is situated on undulating land where there are views northwards to Glastonbury Tor and eastwards to King Alfred's

Tower. Its Blue Lias has been quarried to provide the stone used for many buildings in central Somerset. Its church, which stands in a field at the south of the village has a Norman font and 13th century chancel, but was largely rebuilt in 1800.

The village's outstanding claim to fame is as the birthplace of Henry Brodribb in 1838, better known as Sir Henry Irving, the celebrated actor. He did much to raise the status of the theatre and set out to prove that acting could be an honourable vocation. He was particularly remembered for his roles as Hamlet, Macbeth, Shylock, Wolsey, Lear and Mathias, and was the first actor to achieve a knighthood. He was buried in Westminster Abbey, which perhaps explains why a guidebook of 1912 considered it important to remember that a 'great star in the dramatic firmament rose from the obscurity of a Somerset village.' A solid, grey stone house in the village proudly displays a plaque commemorating this theatrical connection.

Kilve

The pleasant village of Kilve, to the east of East Quantoxhead, straggles its way down a lane off the A39 towards 'Kilve's delightful shore' of Wordsworth's happy recollection. A brook known as Kilve's Pill wends its way alongside, through the village, past the church and ruined chantry to Kilve's 'green sea' as recollected by Southey, another poet.

Squat and unpretentious, the church of St Mary possesses a Norman font, but was restored at the end of the last century. Kilve Chantry was founded in 1329 by Simon de Furneaux with endowed lands for the upkeep of the building and 5 priests, stipulating that prayers should henceforth be offered for himself, his wife and his ancestors. This arrangement was somewhat short lived, for it was dissolved before the end of that century, although the buildings continued to be used. The place, reputed to be a favourite haunt of smugglers, was burnt down in 1848 when timbers and kegs encouraged the flames.

Remains of an old lime kiln and derelict buildings dating from around 1914 when attempts were made to extract shale oil can be seen down on the shore. Ammonites found in the region are referred to as 'St Keyna's serpents', for that saint is said to have turned all serpents to stone in this part of Somerset, and the fossils bear a certain resemblance to coiled snakes.

The tradition of 'glatting' was carried out on these shores, when high spring tides would leave conger eels stranded on the rocky ledges along the beach. There was all the primitive excitement of fox hunting, with shouting and thrashing and barking as men and boys armed with truncheons spattered mud and water about and trained dogs rushed in for the kill as the luckless creatures writhed in desperation. Perhaps with this tradition in the subconscious there was a saying in these parts that a baby born on the high tide would die on an ebb tide.

King's Brompton Common, ***see*** **Clatworthy**

Kingsbury Episcopi

Kingsbury Episcopi has a magnificent church, beautifully proportioned, with a typical Somerset tower which reaches a height of 100 feet above the moors. The handsome tower, which can be viewed to good effect against a flat landscape and wide skyscape bears witness to the faith and genius of Somerset's early craftsmen.

This delightful Ham stone village on the Parrett, set in an area of willows and buttercup meadows to the south of Muchelney, derives its stylish name from having been an ancient possession of the Bishopric (Bishop's Kingsbury). A cottage near the church dates from the 16th century, and near the Wesleyan chapel, built in 1810, is the old village lock-up, an octagonal building capped with an ornate finial.

Kingsdon, ***see*** **Charlton Mackrell**

Kingston St Mary

Taunton Vale is rich in 'dragon' folklore, which may have been derived by Authurian legend or from struggles between West Wales and Wessex, where dragon standards were carried. A dragon, reputedly slaughtered at Kingston St Mary is depicted on the pastoral staff of the Bishop of Bath and Wells.

Another fiery visitor to the village in 1766 was John Wesley, who regarded the vicarage as being 'just right for a contemplative man'. A man who helped him in his contemplations was the curate of South Petherton, Dr Coke, who, fired with enthusiasm adopted a similarly compelling style, and having been relieved of his curacy on account of this devoted his time to wayside preaching here and in America.

The village, situated to the north of Taunton on the southern edges of the Quantocks in a traditional area of cider growing, gave its name to an old fashioned cider apple. The 'Kingston Black' was reputed to produce 'a sweet, slightly sharp, full cider of a pleasant and fruity flavour'. In former times labourers' scant wages were supplemented with an inferior brew known as 'second wringing', and they brought along their firkins to be filled.

The village's crowning glory is its church, with its lofty pinnacled tower showing up particularly well against its wooded Quantock background. It is regarded as 'among the great masterpieces of English architecture', and reflects the wealth once generated by the cloth industry.

Nearby Hestercombe House is particularly admired for the beauty of its setting, where nature and art are so pleasingly blended. Having been in the possession of the Warre family for 600 years, the house has now been taken over by Somerset County Council for its Fire Brigade Headquarters. The gardens were laid out by Edward Lutyens and Gertrude Jekyll.

A character who has apparently not been seen off by the local dragons is Old Mr Surtees, who, on Old Christmas Eve, is said to ride his phantom white horse down nearby Tainfield Drive to an accompaniment of rattling chains and eerie noises. Local folk of a philosophical turn of mind used to chant:

'Mr Surtees, he wobbled the knees,
All on a Saturday night!'

After the church service on Whit Monday, it was customary for the village folk to wear blue sashes (which usually denoted temperance) and carry staffs for their procession through the village. This was the prelude to a day of pleasurable diversions in the open air, with a band providing the music. There would be sports, contests and refreshments with dancing in the evening. Energetic folk took part in the traditional walk from the Farmer's Arms to Bishop's Lydeard.

Kingstone, *see* Dowlish Wake

Knole, *see* Long Sutton

Langford Budville

The River Tone meanders its peaceful way through the lovely borderland countryside to the west of Wellington, separating the villages of Langford Budville and Thorne St Margaret. On Midsummer Night the churchbells of Langford Budville were rung to drive the Devil over to Thorne St Margaret; a gesture which was enthusiastically reciprocated on St Becket's Day (July 7th), when Thorne St Margaret's bells returned the compliment. Perhaps this unrest has some influence on the ghostly hunting squire who periodically makes desperate attempts to ride home to Norton Manor from Langford Budville — but never makes it.

It is said in these parts that ash trees have healing powers — for those willing to take a chance. To cure a child of hernia split an ash and arrange for 2 women to pass the sick child through the gap 7 times before sunrise, then bind up the division in the tree with hazel bands. The fate of the tree thereafter will be the fate of the child, for if the tree is mutilated, the child will also suffer.

The craftsman who designed and executed the stone needle and thread on one of the stone columns in the church cleverly set people puzzling and pondering down the ages. Thread is certainly easier to get through the eye of a needle than a camel, and of course everyone knows what a stitch in time saves. What was that old saying about needles and pins and troubles beginning when a man marries? Equally sexist and unpopular in some quarters is the theory that a woman must have built the church. Whimsical theories will no doubt continue, but it is genuinely thought to have some connection with the age old custom at Queen's College, Oxford, whereby Fellows and undergraduates are presented with a needle and thread on New Year's Day in accordance with the founder's bequest.

Nearby Cothay Manor, in its serene and beautiful setting by the River Tone, is considered to be one of the most perfect 15th century manor houses in Britain, with its great hall, solar and minstrels' galleries in their original state.

Laverton

The woollen trade flourished in Frome in the 18th century and the spinning of wool was carried out by women and children in the town and surrounding villages, including Laverton Master. Clothiers went around each week distributing the wool and collecting the spun yarn.

Laverton, on secondary roads to the north of Frome, and on the course of Wheel Brook, has an interesting church which has Norman windows and a Jacobean loft with balustrading reminiscent of that in the Bishop's Palace at Wells. Amongst its rectors in the 18th century was William Keate, father of John, who became a noteworthy headmaster of Eton College, and Robert, who was a member of the council of the College of Surgeons for many years and three times its president.

Manor Farm, to the north of the church has attractive mullioned windows, a fine, vaulted plaster ceiling dated 1627 and a large, interesting fireplace. This place was visited on 23rd June 1909 by the Prince and Princess of Wales (later King George and Queen Mary), who witnessed the complete process of Cheddar cheese making.

Leigh-on-Mendip

This pleasant, but rather bleak and straggling upland stone village, formerly known as Lye under Mendyp, once supplied a local need by producing handles for spades and shovels fashioned from ash from the local timber mill. However, its main claim to fame is its church of St Giles, whose noble tower is regarded as one of the finest in Somerset. When the church was built, Leigh was part of the manor and parish of Mells, owned by Glastonbury Abbey.

Just to the south , in the village of Downhead, the church of All Saints has eight fantastic gargoyles leering down from the tower, which has diagonal buttresses, battlements and pinnacles.

Limington

To the east of the Roman town of Ilchester, and in the valley of the Yeo is the village of Limington, remembered for its connections with Cardinal Wolsey. Thomas Wolsey, born at Ipswich ('an honest poor man's son'), graduated from Oxford at the age of 15 and was destined to become Archbishop of York and Cardinal of Rome. Having acted as tutor to the Earl of Dorset's sons, the Earl presented him with the living at Limington, (*see* Lopen and Hinton St George).

Sir Amyas Poulett, High Sheriff of Somerset, was to rue the day he authorised the placing of young Thomas in the stocks after he had celebrated a little too well at Lopen fair; for how was he to know that the student was destined to become one of the most powerful figures in the land? Wolsey never forgot the humiliating incident, and as Chancellor of England he turned the tables by placing his tormentor under a Tudor style version of house arrest for 'five or six years or more.'

In the chapel of the church, originally a chantry founded in 1329, are effigies of its founder Sir Richard Gyverney, lord of the manor, depicted cross legged and in chain mail, his wife and 2 other figures.

Little Load, *see* Long Load

Litton

Around the Mendip village of Litton, with its neat and trim stone cottages lining the steep streets, witches were credited with the ability to come down chimneys, allowing them to gain unwelcome entry into unsuspecting folks' homes. This potential hazard needed to be guarded against, and thus bullocks' hearts stuffed full of outward projecting pins were suspended in chimneys as protective charms.

The pure nature of the local water, which has long attracted attention, was ideal for paper making at the village mill, and as far back as 1845 the water from Sherborne Springs was harnessed as part of an on-going scheme for providing water for the city of Bristol.

Long Load

Before 1795, canal craft were able to come up the River Parrett on the tide to a point just below Langport. In that year plans were approved for the Ilchester and Langport Navigation Company to develop the system beyond Langport to Long Load and Ilchester, but the project was never fully completed. Long Load became for some time the port serving Martock, Yeovil and southern Somerset.

Today the village extends for about a mile alongside the B3165 to the narrow, medieval bridge spanning the River Yeo where modern day traffic is controlled by lights. On the northern side of the river at Little Load there are traces of the former wharf.

Long Sutton

An old humpbacked bridge over the River Yeo carries present day traffic northwards from Long Load to Long Sutton, which quartered Goring and the Royalist troops before the Battle of Langport, and Fairfax and his men after their defeat. This place, which in Saxon times is recorded as possessing an 'enclosure where beans grow', is particularly notable for its handsome church, built around 1490 with a lofty tower similar in style to those of Langport and Huish Episcopi. Other architectural gems in this village include the 17th century manor house just south of the church, the 17th century Court House and the pleasingly proportioned Friends' Meeting House, dating from 1717, situated to the north of the village on a corner adjoining the A372. The manor possesses a 16th century barn and medieval dovecot.

The Devonshire Arms looks out approvingly across the pretty, tree dotted village green, flanked by the church of the Holy Trinity, the school and other attractive buildings connected with the quiet hub of village life. It is pleasant to take a leisurely stroll along the lanes to the attractive hamlet of Knole, to the east of the village.

Lopen

Not very many places can claim the distinction of having had one of our greatest clerical statesmen confined in their village stocks, but Lopen is able to do just this; for Thomas Wolsey, son of an Ipswich butcher, was destined to become Archbiship of York and Cardinal of Rome. At the time of this particlar escapade he was engaged as a tutor to the sons of the Earl of Dorset. However, having entered into the spirit of the famous Lopen Fair with rather too much enthusiasm, he was confined to the stocks by Sir Amyas Poulett for disorderly conduct; a decision for which Poulett was to pay dearly in the years to come (*see* Limington).

Lopen Fair existed at the beginning of the 13th century and became a seven day Whitsun event renowned for its diversity of attractions — including feasting and drinking, wrestling, cudgelling and single sticking, as well as the brightly decorated stalls which offered a tempting array of goods. The site of the old fair was around the Cross Tree in the centre of the village, and a fragment of the partly submerged medieval cross shaft remains there today opposite the Old Bakehouse. The fair suffered as a result of competition from nearby Hinton St George, but in common with that village they celebrated Halloween as 'Punkie Night'.

Lopen Head, at the north of the village, originally known as White Cross, was on the Western mailcoach route of the early 19th century and had an inn with horse changing facilities. The village is dissected by the Fosse Way Roman road, and had a brook to the south harnessed by mills which were let to tenants for life in the earliest times. Apart from agriculture there was a quarry and limekiln and employment in the textile industry. Cloth, sailcloth, sail twine, rope and twine were manufactured in the village and there were bleaching grounds and a rope walk. Weaving died out towards the end of the last century, but rope and twine production continued until after the First World War. During the war the industry was taken over by the Board of Agriculture and Fisheries, and the Government constructed a new plant in the Second World War.

Low Ham

Remains of one of the best examples of a Roman villa were discovered at Low Ham, to the north of Langport. Planned around a courtyard, with an elaborate system of bath houses, it had a fine mosaic floor depicting scenes from the Aeneid, including the story of Dido and Aeneas.

The very unusual church, which stands in a green field without a churchyard, was built by Sir Edward Hext in 1650 in imitation Gothic style and has an embattled west tower. It was built as a private chapel to the big house, which was never finished, owing to the fate of Sir John Stawell (*see* Cothelstone). The gates were removed to Hazelgrove House, at Sparkford.

Lower Chillington, *see* Chillington

Luccombe

This picturesque, secluded little village to the south east of Porlock was a particular delight to Wordsworth and Coleridge. It derives its name from its closed situation in a combe, beside the watercourse.

The area, which is a delight to walkers and those who love unspoilt countryside, is rich in evidence of prehistory. The expert eye can pick out the pattern of the Iron Age field systems which are shown on the Ordnance Survey maps. Small, rectangular arable fields were divided by banks and low ridges, which would have been topped by hedges to keep wild and domestic animals away from the crops.

St Mary's church has a fine waggon roof and slender tower. There is a mural tablet in the church to the Royalist rector Henry Byam, who was born and died in the village. During the Civil War he gathered together a band of local recruits for the king, putting four of his sons in command of them.

Horner Water cascades its delightful way down from Dunkery Beacon through the wooded combes and on past Horner, which derives its name from 'hwrnur', said to mean snorer. But there's no time for snoring, particularly after the rains when the water has built up. The story goes that a rider who was thrown into the water in time of flood was swiftly swept downsteam in front of horrified and helpless onlookers, and that his body was eventually recovered from the sea off Bossington.

This enchanting area is particularly interesting for its wildlife, and the Holnicote Estate has now been taken over by the National Trust. Just northwards of Horner is West Luccombe, where a lovely old packhorse bridge crosses Horner Water.

As in other remote places around the county, there was a real fear of witches and witchcraft in the area. Eccentric old ladies were watched closely for significant signs revealing their true nature, and the most innocent of actions, gestures or habits were seized upon as evidence of being grey or black witches. Counter charms, usually consisting of crossed pins were strategically placed in an effort to protect innocent folk from their mischief. As well as warding off bad luck, there were ways of attracting good fortune. On Easter Sunday it was worth the effort of getting up very early and walking to the top of Dunkery Beacon in time to see the sun rise, as this was regarded as a kind of insurance policy for the next 12 months. On the last day of April, more romantically known as May Eve, farming folk placed primroses in the cattle stalls and garlanded the stable doors. On this night villagers would hang evergreen branches over the thresholds last thing at night before retiring to bed. Many country places have variations on these deep rooted symbolic themes.

Lufton, *see* Montacute

Lullington

To the north east of Frome, the lovely village of Lullington stands on a knoll rising from the watermeadows. Its Norman church of All Saints was described by Dr Nikolaus Pevsner as 'perhaps the most enjoyable Norman village church in Somerset,' and by Arthur Mee as a 'gem of England'. Praise indeed.

The earliest Norman churches were strong, massive structures of stern simplicity. This church reflects the transitional period from Norman to Early English, when the art of decoration was just beginning to emerge. Thus Lullington's church is remarkable and in many respects unique. The decorated Norman doorways are a delight, even to those who have little understanding or appreciation of the finer points of church architecture. The interesting font is the most highly decorated Norman font in the county.

The gateway from Lullingstone to Orchardleigh Park keeps us still in the land of superlatives, for:

> 'What a peace steals over me
> Born of happy memory;
> Lullington and Orchardleigh.'

This is the romantic Orchardleigh Park with the 'old broken manor of the Champneys and the island church therein'. St Mary's church on its island in the middle of the lake was restored in 1879 in sympathy with its age and small size. The new house was constructed between 1855 and 1858 in the Elizabethan style. Also in the park are two standing stones, which are the remains of a chambered long barrow.

The poet Henry Newbolt, who described Orchardleigh in his historical romance *The Old Country* using the name 'Gardenleigh', is buried here.

Luxborough

Somerset is certainly a county of contrasts and amazing diversity in the many faces it presents. Luxborough is a lonely outpost high in the Brendon Hills in an area rich in minerals, and bearing evidence of much prehistoric activity. From this wild and windy place there are superb views, particularly to the north west over Croydon Hill to the sea.

Metal and coal were exploited in this part of the Brendons in the 16th century, and in the 19th century there was another short but intense burst of industrial activity. Iron ore was produced around Luxborough in the early 1840's and by 1853 mining activity had extended to Raleigh's Cross and Gupworthy (*see* Gupworthy). The West Somerset Mineral Line took the ore to the port of Watchet, from whence it was shipped to South Wales to supply the Ebbw Vale iron and steel works.

Welsh and Cornish miners were enticed into the area and at first the men lodged at local farms and cottages. The mining company built settlements for their workers, including one at Brendon Hill near Raleigh's Cross, where there was a coal depot, general stores, temperance hotel and 3 places of worship. These purpose-built places were run according to the policy of the company, and there was a strong Noncomformist and teetotal bias. Social life revolved around the Temperance Society, Teetotal Fife and Drum Band, a Band of Hope and a choir.

Between 1880 and 1890 the price of ore fell, the miners drifted away and the buildings and machinery fell into disuse. Further attempts to renew the industry were made in the early part of this century, but they were abandoned by 1911 and the tracks were removed at the beginning of the First World War for munitions. Thus a fascinating insight into industrial archaeology lurks just beneath the undergrowth, until someone decides to expose part of our heritage for everyone to wonder at, or possibly further attempts are made to exploit the wealth lying dormant in the hills.

Lympsham, *see* Brent Knoll

Lytes Cary, *see* Charlton Mackrell

Mark, *see* Wedmore

Marston Bigot, *see* **Nunney**

Marston Magna

Streams rising in the hilly landscape of the Somerset and Dorset border country converge to flow through the village of Marston Magna, before joining the River Yeo to the west of Chilton Cantelo. One of the few branch lines to survive, which links Weymouth with Castle Cary, runs close by. The brook, which operated a mill in the first part of this century also formed part of the moat in an area now known as Court Garden. This may originally have been the site of a bishop's palace or possibly of a grange house of the Polshoe nunnery.

Set on a bank above the brook is the church of late 11th century origin, but mainly dating from the 13th and 14th centuries. It has a 3 storey embattled west tower with a clock of 6 bells. Formerly there was a clock erected in 1710, made by William Monk, who also made the clock for Sherborne Abbey.

To the south west of the church is the long, low, mellow toned 17th century manor house. Some of the buildings in the village have dripstones on the windows and bear evidence of having been incorporated in earlier structures. There are some noteworthy almshouses.

Martock

The delightful little town of Martock with a village-like charm is constructed almost entirely of Ham Hill stone, mellowed to a pleasing soft, golden tone. Its fine, 13th century church of All Saints has a splendid timber roof with seven hundred and fifty carved panels, mostly of individual design, said to be the finest in Somerset. This was the church where Cromwell and Fairfax and their troops gave thanks in 1645 for the taking of Bridgwater.

In the middle of the village, opposite the church is the 13th and 14th century Treasurer's House with its medieval hall and kitchen and fine collar braced timber roof, so called because the vicar of Martock was once Treasurer of Wells Cathedral. Rating as one of the oldest inhabited houses in the country, it is now in the care of the National

Trust and can be viewed by appointment with the tenant.

Church House, formerly the old Court House, was once the Grammar School, founded by William Strode of Barrington in 1661 for 'schollers of the towne and hundred'. The school which taught Hebrew, Latin and Greek, chose for its motto 'Neglect not thy opportunities'. Other buildings of interest are the ruined, moated manor house, the 17th century manor house, the Market House and the market cross with its ancient base and fluted column crowned with a sundial and ball finial. It marks the spot where an ancient oak tree once grew, and around which the market and fair were held. The name 'Martock' is said to be derived from 'Market Oak', and it used to be described as 'Martock inter Aquas', meaning situated on land between the rivers Ivel and Parrett.

Martock, close to the former river port of Little Load was originally dependent on agriculture, and in the 18th century there was a rather earthy saying 'take a Martock man by the collar and shake him, and you will hear the beans rattle in his belly'. In the absence of a local estate to dominate the economy, local farmers were able to grow 'fat in their purses'. It was said that they enjoyed the wealth being generated, but lacked the manners and breeding which usually went with it. However, as the clothing and manufacturing industries evolved in the 18th and 19th centuries wealthy families were able to give their children a good education, thereby giving rise to opportunities in more 'upmarket' trades and in the professions.

The emergence of the merchant and professional classes paved the way to a good social life in Martock with opportunities for trade, commercial and cultural pursuits. In 1911 money was raised to build a hangar for D.G. Gilmour, who was 'the first airman to fly an aeroplane over this part of the country'.

Meare

Between the low hills of Wedmore and the Polden ridge is the village of Meare, situated on a low island projecting above the surrounding moors. It is thought to have derived its name from the days when it was a lake pond or 'mere', before the successive drainage operations claimed large areas of land.

This was one of the Iron Age lake settlements (*see* Godney and

Westhay). The earliest excavations of Meare and Godney lake villages in the 1890s revealed the settlements, well preserved in the peat. Sophisticated scientific techniques can now date the sequences in peat levels, revealing changes in the climate as well as the developing pattern of social changes among these early settlers. A pot dated at 2,000 BC was discovered in Meare Heath.

It is thought that the settlement at Meare differed from that at Godney in that it was built on raised peat which had dried at the water's edge, rather than on a re-inforced stilt-like structure in the water. Some of the hut foundations were rectangular as well as oval. However, emerging scientific evidence is subject to variations in its interpretation thereby throwing doubt on formerly accepted theories as well as on new ones; a situation confusing for the layman and difficult for writers of history. The up-to-date theory veers towards the Glastonbury lake villages being lakeside settlements. Interesting discoveries can be viewed at the County Museum, Taunton.

Meare, the Abbot's Fish House

This area, 'the immense turbary' dominated by Glastonbury Tor, is popularly regarded as the Avalon of Arthurian legend. The monks of Glastonbury claimed to possess the mortal remains of King Arthur and his queen; a claim which increased their revenue whether it could be proved or not. Glastonbury and its ruined abbey has always been steeped in legend and romance. Some say that the name 'Avalon' was derived from Avallach, which was the Celtic realm of the Dead, others associate it rather more pleasantly with the 'land of apples' or 'the apple orchard'.

The former Meare Pool, once the fish preserve of the abbots of Glastonbury extended for 500 acres in Elizabethan times and was drained in 1712. The unique and intriguing abbey Fish House once stored salted fish, tackle and equipment downstairs and housed the fish bailiff in the upper storey. Today, the Fish House, abbots' manor house and the church with its low tower create a scene of pleasing 14th century charm in their meadowland setting.

Drainage schemes of Somerset's lowlands, operated by the great religious houses of Glastonbury, Athelney, Wells and Muchelney resulted in unholy squabbles over boundaries, fishing rights and the digging of peat.

Today, Meare stands above the marshes which echo to the call of the wildfowl, while Glastonbury Tor, capped with its romantic ruin stands sentinel.

Mells

'Little Jack Horner
Sat in a corner
Eating a Christmas pie;
He put in a thumb
And pulled out a plum
And said 'What a brave boy am I."

Popular folklore would have it that Jack, one of the Horners of Mells, formerly the Abbot of Glastonbury's steward at the time of the dissolution of the monasteries, was sent to try and placate Thomas Cromwell with a bribe in the form of a pie, in a desperate attempt to save the abbey. But this was no ordinary pie, for under the pastry lay the title deeds of 12 of the abbey's manors. During the course of carrying out his errand, Jack, who was feeling rather greedy, lifted the piecrust and carefully extricated the metaphorical plum . . . the deeds of the manor of Mells. Although this nursery rhyme might imply that acquiring an estate was as easy as pie, it was not really quite like that. In fact legal documents relating to the transaction are still in existence; no such culinary art was employed, and we have to concede that this was a cooked-up story.

The delightful village of Mells which lies to the north west of

Frome, is a showpiece, inclined to cause visitors and writers to wax lyrical. The historian Leland wrote: 'Melles hath bene a praty Townelet of Clothing. It longgid unto Glessenbryi. The church is faire and builid in tyme of mynde ex lapide quadrato by the hole Paroche. Ther is a praty Maner Place of Stone harde at the West Ende of the Chirche. This be likelihod was partely builded by Abbate Selwoode of Glasteinbyri syns it servid the Farmer of the Lordeship. Now Mr Horner hath boute the Lordeship of the King'. A guidebook of the 1920's stated: 'Mells, the very name of which is sweet (Parochia mellis), lies in a valley thick with trees and musical with bees and the sound of running water'.

This village, with its pleasing stone cottages, 15th century church, Elizabethan manor and 15th century Talbot Inn, set against greens and trees, also has connections with mining and quarrying. Fussells, the iron masters were making edged tools as far back as 1744. Their success led to mills being constructed in neighbouring villages, a situation which caused conflict and legal battles with Jack Horner's landowning descendants. The company, which exported agricultural tools widely, was awarded Gold medals for their scythes and realhooks at the Exhibition of Vienna in 1860. The industry fell into decline, and today the evidence lies in the dams along the watercourses, and derelict structures beneath the undergrowth.

Merriott

Unofficially dubbed 'Little Ireland' on account of the villagers' dark hair, swarthy complexion and distinctive dialect, the good folk of Merriott near Crewkerne were naturally logical when it came to sorting out the confusion caused by a shortage of surnames; they invented nicknames such as Boneback, Curlhead and Noghead.

The potential of Merriott's rich and fertile soil was recognised from the earliest times when the ancient woodlands were cleared to produce the open, arable fields of the Middle Ages. The local tradition of gardening pre-dates 1370 when references were made to 'a tree nursery'. Throughout the ages the place has been a gardeners' delight, producing fruit, root crops and every kind of vegetable, and was particularly suited to the growing of hemp and flax for the textile industry. Cottagers, who also kept bees, would be helped by their wives and families, and husbands went around the countryside selling their produce. Webbers, who ran the well known nursery and who were somewhat ahead of their time in producing catalogues, sold out to John Scott in 1852. Scotts Nurseries continue to flourish today.

At the time of Domesday there were four mills. Court Mill ground to a halt shortly before the Second World War and Billings Mill, formerly Berdons Mill at the western end of the village, worked until the early 1960's. Other occupations included weaving, fulling and dyeing and the making of tobacco pipes, sailcloth, rope and gloves. The village suffered a devastating fire in 1811 which destroyed twenty-four cottages.

Law and order was all important in 16th century Merriott, when, it was declared, 'thieves ought to be hanged at the gallows', and the playing of unlawful games or non-attendance at church could land villagers in their pillory or stocks. A round, tiled lock-up constructed of Ham Hill stone was later erected near Manor Farm. In the 18th century only church going, badge-wearing paupers were entitled to benefit and in the 19th century the churchwardens busied themselves raising money for the emigration of paupers. Although active involvement with the church was all important, there were some strange goings on beneath that respectable canopy. In the 16th and 17th centuries church treasures were sold without consent, a churchwarden was accused of serving up 'alehouse beer' in the communion cup and a curate became so drunk that 'he would have cut off some of his hand to give his dog.'

Today older folk recall the old bakehouses in Merriott, one of which continued with horse and cart delivery until after the last war. There is still a flourishing social life within this pleasant, friendly, neat and very clean village.

Middlezoy

Middlezoy is one of the villages on a ridge of silty ground on the edge of Sedgemoor, once known as the 'Island of Sowy'. In former times much of this area was covered by water or marshland with connecting causeways. 'Zoy' denotes an island, while names ending in 'oy' indicated settlements on such islands.

The migrant West Saxon herdsmen or 'Somersaetas' (summer dwellers), brought their flocks to graze here after the spring floods had receded, uncovering the causeways and exposing the succulent, new growth of grass.

When the village belonged to Glastonbury Abbey, the Lord Abbot was entitled to a third of the catch from these fishing grounds. However, tenants were encouraged to drain their land as part of the reclamation project. In 1238 the land was graded into marsh, mow, pasture and meadow, and having upgraded their land they then had to pay taxes on a higher grade. Middlezoy was the richest of the Abbot's holdings throughout the Levels.

Fairfax and Cromwell were here with their forces in July 1645 following the Battle of Langport and prior to the storming of Bridgwater. Inside the church is a brass memorial to Louis Chevalier de Misiers, a Frenchman who fought for the Royalists and lost his life at Sedgemoor in July 1685. The church with its massive tower dominates the landscape over the marshes.

Midelney Manor, *see* Curry Rivel

Milborne Port

Milborne Port, just inside the Somerset border to the north east of Sherborne, knew early importance and derived its name from being a port — or market — on the millstream. It was a Royal Manor and had a mint between 997 and 1007.

By 1086 it had become a borough, prosperous from the cloth making industry, with mills working busily around the area, and representatives were sent to Parliament in the days of Edward I. However, it was to become disenfranchised as a rotten borough in 1832, although its cloth making and leather industry continued to prosper.

The church, dating from Saxon times, has a fine Norman doorway and an exceptionally beautiful and delicate 15th century screen with the carving for its roodloft on a canopy. At the time of the Rebellion, Milborne Port was occupied by some of Cromwell's men who stole the Bible from the church. This deed so angered the inhabitants that they drove the soldiers out of the town.

Somerset folk have long been wary of cursing, fearing the effects it might bring. A workhouse woman of Milborne Port who used the blasphemous 'God strike me dead!' in 1813 achieved her wish and was instantly struck down dead. On Shrove Tuesday or 'Pan Shard

Night' the youngsters paraded around the town in search of pots and pans with which to bombard doors. Having thus obtained the hardware, they visited folks' homes chanting:

'Flitter me, flatter me, Floor,
If you don't give me some pancakes,
I'll beat down your door!'

Today the church, the old Guildhall and the large and imposing Ven House with their outstanding architecture remind us of a once glorious past. Things are rather quieter around Milborne Port these days.

Templecombe, 3 miles to the north east consists of 2 parts, Abbas Combe and the Temple Combe, which derived its name from the Knights Templar who had a chapel there, founded in the 12th century by Serlo Fitz-Odo.

Misterton

Misterton, shortened from Minsterton (referring to the Mother Church at Crewkerne) owes its existence to its position on the early trading routes near the turnpikes. Life was geared to communications and the needs of travellers and this gave rise to the large number of inns including the White Swan, later known as the Swan, the George, the Four Alls, the New Inn, the Globe Inn and the Masons' Arms. Its inclusion in the railway network in 1860, close to the outlying Crewkerne Station gave it a further boost, opening up opportunities for coal, timber, slate and agricultural merchants and others. The Queen's Hotel, adjacent to the station opened in 1886.

Today Misterton lies in an area scheduled for expansion, and the new industrial estates here and around Crewkerne offer further opportunities for development.

The place has literary associations for Helen Mathers (1853-1920), author of *Comin' Through The Rye* and other novels was born here and wrote here, while the Rev Arthur Collier (1680-1732) who wrote on metaphysics and religion, inherited an estate here.

The artist Knighton Hammond, one of this country's leading water colourists, came to live here and paint the Dorset and Somerset scene, having spent much of his life as an artist in France and Italy.

Monksilver

The village lies in a deep valley among the Brendon foothills, clustered around its 15th century church to the south of Watchet. In the churchyard lie Elizabeth Conibeer and her 2 daughters, victims of the notorious 'Monksilver Murderer' in the 18th century. The murder case was never officially solved, but some local people were aware of the murderer's identity and it was generally thought to have been a 'blood letting' ritual to break a spell, which went wrong. Their tombstone inscription reads:

'Inhuman wretch, whoe'er thou art
That didst commit this horrid crime
Repent before thou dost depart
To meet thy awful Judge Divine.'

It is very unlucky to catch sight of the strange light which sometimes appears around the murder spot.

Nearby Combe Sydenham was the home of Drake's wife Elizabeth Sydenham. The lovers had promised faithfully to be true before Sir Francis sailed away on a lengthy voyage. However, Elizabeth's overbearing father Sir George was determined to get her comfortably married off to a wealthy suitor and the marriage plans went ahead despite her protests. As the bridal party reached the door of the church, a red hot 'cannon ball', thought to have been fired by Sir Francis, dropped from the heavens to land among them. The marriage did not take place, despite the fact that the 'cannon-ball' was in reality a meteorite, which remained in the village as a trophy. If anyone attempted to take it away, it was said to return inexplicably to its rightful place. As for Sir George, he lies buried in Stogumber churchyard, but his ghost still rides a galloping horse along the valley.

Montacute

The elegant Ham Hill stone village of Montacute which lies about 4 miles to the west of Yeovil, and reflects its former importance in its handsome buildings, derives its name from the Latin 'mons acutus' referring to a pointed hill. The hill in question was the conical St Michael's Hill, now topped with a folly tower. The village extends to the south and east of the church, and there are some pleasing 17th and 18th century houses in the main square known as The Borough.

In the 7th century the settlement lying at the base of this steep hill was known as Logworesbeorh, having been named after a monk of Glastonbury, and it later became known as Bishopston after one Abbot of Glastonbury became Bishop of Winchester.

Back in the days of King Canute, it is said that the village blacksmith had a dream that the Holy Cross was hidden in St Michael's Hill. When the miraculous relic was unearthed, Torfig, the lord of the manor, placed it on a wagon to be drawn by 12 white cows and 12 red oxen to a place to be divinely directed. A list of English shrines was chanted and at the name of Walton the beasts set out spontaneously on their quest to found an abbey. In Norman times the Count of Mortain, half brother of William the Conqueror, erected a castle on the much favoured spot.

Robert, Earl of Mortain, who had connections with the French Cluniac Priory of St Peter and St Paul founded Montacute Priory which was endowed with a castle, a borough, vineyards, orchards, a mill and later a park. The place grew in importance and by 1306 it was sending 2 representatives to Parliament. In the Middle Ages it was a prosperous market town, but by the 16th century it began to decline, partly from the competition from Ilminster and Yeovil which were better placed on busy routes. By the end of the 18th century it had declined to a village.

The magnificent Elizabethan mansion of Montacute House, constructed of the honey coloured Ham Hill stone to an 'H' shaped ground plan is one of the finest houses of the South West. Built by the Phelips family, and now in the care of the National Trust it contains a valuable collection of furniture, china, portraits and tapestry and has interesting plasterwork and panelling.

The church of St Catherine has an early Norman chancel and 16th century monuments to the Phelips family. A one time vicar was the father of the literary Powys brothers, who spent some of their formative years here.

There is a Roman villa to the west on Hamden Hill, and a late Romano-British corridor house was discovered to the east at Lufton in 1945 when a field was being ploughed. Its main feature was an elaborate bath suite with a pyramid roof, surrounded by a graceful fishy mosaic.

Moorlinch

Moorlinch or Moorlynch, lies just west of Greinton, along the middle of the southern flank of the Polden Hills, close to the Greylake Fosse, which was an early link across Sedgemoor with the 'Sowy' villages. Moorlinch was one of the sister parishes which squabbled about a legacy of churchbells. To the particular embarrassment of Stawell, Moorlinch won! (*see* Stawell).

Swayne, the Sedgemoor rebel, is said to have had the useful knack of evading his captors by his impressive ability to make gigantic leaps. The stones here, known as Swayne's Jumps recall his prowess for posterity. Moorlinch commands fine views over the former battlefield, now a pleasing and tranquil moorland scene of rhines, cultivations and pastures, in a distinctive landscape dotted with handsome church towers.

The church of St Mary has a broad, low unbuttressed west tower of the late 13th century. An effigy of a lady with a detailed head dress dates from around 1375. In the churchyard there is a broken shaft and base of an old cross.

Greinton, with its stone built houses and farms, has a church which still contains some 12th century work in its south door.

Muchelney

Muchelney lies just south of Langport on the River Parrett and is a little village of great interest and quiet charm. Although its name denotes a 'big island', it is actually rather small. Its protected situation between the rivers Parrett and Yeo, with surrounding marshland, rendered it suitable as the site of one of the most important places of the Somerset Levels. For a Benedictine abbey, said to have been founded by the Wessex King Ine, was built on this section of higher ground amidst the moor and marshland. Next to Glastonbury it was the oldest religious house in Somerset, and the abbey became one of the great ecclesiastical establishments of the Middle Ages. In the 10th century the abbey was re-founded by Athelstan as an act of repentance for having executed his brother Edwin in the mistaken belief that he was plotting to murder him. At the time of Domesday the abbey possessed an acre of vineyard and 2 fisheries yielding 6,000 eels a year. In the 13th century Muchelney, as well as Glastonbury and Athelney, were organising drainage and land reclamation schemes. After the dissolution of the monasteries the place fell into gradual ruin, with stone robbing for building the church and nearby houses.

Foundations of the abbey church can be seen in the churchyard of the parish church next to the handsome Abbots House. The late medieval Priest's House, with its large Gothic hall window, was originally the residence of the secular priests serving the parish church. Now in the care of the National Trust, the hall and parlour can be viewed by written appointment with the tenant.

One priestly anecdote concerns a lady of superior birth and the lowly younger son of an impoverished household who were parted by the lady's parents. Having been falsely told she had married a wealthy man, the lovesick youngster decided to throw his energies into becoming a monk. He was so good at this that he became the Prior of Westover. The lovelorn lady decided to become a nun rather than marry another, and as fate would have it they both ended up in the same religious house. Finding that their love was as strong as ever, they made secret plans to escape. However, for the second time their plans were thwarted by others. He was suddenly whisked away to a far off monastery and she was seized and bricked up in the cellar wall.

In former times trade to Muchelney was by water, for the River Parrett carried traffic up to Langport, where cargo was sometimes unloaded onto smaller barges to be transported to Ilchester or Muchelney.

Drainage schemes continue to evolve, and since the mid 1960s pumping stations on the upper reaches of the Parrett have helped to drain the area around Muchelney.

Today John Leach, grandson of the master potter Bernard Leach whose Orient inspired pots are now collectors' items, carries on the family tradition from his picturesque, thatched workshop to the south of the village.

Neroche Forest, *see* Buckland St Mary, Corfe and Staple Fitzpaine

Nether Stowey

This village on the A39, 10 miles west of Bridgwater, with its restored church, 14th century Stowey Court, delightful 18th century gazebo, unusual timbered clocktower of 1897, Georgian Pole House and attractive houses is much visited by those drawn here for its literary connections.

In 1796 the poet Coleridge, his wife Sara and their son moved to a small thatched cottage in Lime Street, adjoining the garden of their great friend Thomas Poole. This is where the poet wrote *The Rhyme of the Ancient Mariner, Kubla Khan* and the first part of *Christobel,* and it is is now the property of the National Trust. It was Coleridge's friendship with Poole that caused him to move here, and it was Wordsworth's friendship with Coleridge that resulted in Wordsworth and his sister Dorothy moving to nearby Alfoxton (*see* Holford). Fellow writers were drawn to the village, and the close literary kinship which blossomed was viewed with suspicion by the village folk.

The local 'character', Tom Poole, a self taught, cultivated and politically aware tanner, had simple tastes, integrity and showed concern for others, and Coleridge, Wordsworth, Sir Humphry Davy and many leading figures of the time were drawn to this remarkable man.

Today the village is a far cry from John Leland's description of Tudor times: 'Stowey, a poore village stondith yn a Botom, emong Hilles. Heere ys a goodly Maner Place of the Lord Audeley's stonding exceeding pleasauntly for goodly Pastures, and having by it a Parke of redde Deere and another of falow, and a faire Brooke serving al the Offices of the Maner Place. The Lord Audley, that rebellid yn Henry the vij Tyme, began great Foundations of Stone Work to the enlarging of his House, the which yet be seene half onperfect. The Ryver of Stowey risith yn the Hilles thereby by West, and renning along thorough Stowey Village goith after to the Se.'

The castle which formerly stood nearby, a one time property of the Audley family, is now a grass covered ruin. This was originally part of Somerset's 'dragon' country, for a dragon was reputed to live in the woods between Nether Stowey and Holford. It so happened that a weary woodcutter seeking work sat down on a log to rest. When the 'log' reared up and showed itself to be a dragon, the woodcutter had the swift presence of mind to grab his axe and slay the beast with a single blow. Generations of children feared to go near the woods. Probably linked with this legend is the tradition of men and boys hunting Judas in Shervage Wood, where red squirrels represented red haired Judas. Red squirrels today face near extinction throughout most parts of Britain (*see also* Stogursey).

North Cadbury

This large and pleasant village constructed of the grey oolitic limestone widely used hereabouts is separated from South Cadbury, contender for King Arthur's Camelot by the River Cam, and today's busy A303. To the west is the old route linking South Cadbury with Glastonbury, known as 'King Arthur's Hunting Causeway.'.

North Cadbury's splendid church beside the gabled Tudor manor house is considered by many to be the finest complete Perpendicular church in Somerset. It was reconstructed in 1422 by the Botreaux family. The village has had former rectors with the knack of getting their names down in history. John Feron, who died in 1407 achieved this over a century and a half later, when a bell crashed onto his tomb, destroying the inscription about his having 'builded this tower at his owne proper coste'. Following the gift of the patronage of the church to Emmanuel College, Cambridge, at the end of the 16th century, the parish came under strict Puritan influence. Fun and games and folk making merry were all frowned on. The rector complained in 1634 that 'on Midsomer day last in time of Morninge prayer and sermon a company from Gallington . . . came with a Morrice Daunce and with Fidlers and with a drume, and held on theire sports so neere into the Church . . . makinge such a noyse . . .' Despite being twice asked to leave, they carried on with their music and dancing. A rector named Whichcot, who was Provost of King's College, Cambridge, served here from 1643 to 1650. He was succeeded by Ralph Cudworth, one of the most learned of the English divines and philosophers, who penned an intellectual work with a lengthy title which could be a contender for the *Book of Records* (*see* Aller).

North Coker, *see* West Coker

North Curry

The sizable village of North Curry, on the western arm of higher land jutting above the moors to the south of the River Tone was, with Stoke St Gregory, a centre of the withy growing trade, holding withy auctions.

North Curry was a royal manor until 1300, when Richard I gave it to the Dean and Chaper of Wells. The tradition of the Reeves Feast was established during the reign of King John, who had a reputation for many things, but who was popular with Somerset folk and regarded as a fine huntsman. On the Sunday before Christmas the Reeve chose 3 heifers to be put in the manor pound to await Yuletide festivities. He also gathered together other livestock to provide meat as well as obtaining fruit, vegetables and bread. The feast began with the guests entering his house chanting the traditional rhyme. Toasts were proposed to the king and the 2 Jacks who acted as joint masters of ceremonies. For the Feast of King John's Mince Pie on Christmas night, a huge mince pie topped by an effigy of the king was borne aloft in grand style. Two large candles were lit, a toast was proposed to the memory of the monarch, then everyone was free to eat and drink as much as they desired in the time it took for the candles to burn out. There were variations on this theme here and elsewhere in the county, when land would be auctioned to the burning of candles, with proceeds going to the upkeep of the church.

Today North Curry emerges as a village with a neat and prosperous air. The impressive church, set amidst leafy, lofty chestnut trees possesses fine details of the decorated style, has a 13th century tower, a beautiful Norman north doorway and has earned the name 'the Cathedral of the Moors'.

North Petherton

North Petherton, together with Exmoor, Selwood, Mendip and Neroche was originally one of the great medieval hunting forests of Somerset, incorporating the monastery at Athelney, founded by King Alfred. The forests, which were not necessarily covered by trees, were subject to very strict laws which were much resented by local folk who formerly had rights enabling them to hunt for food. North Petherton Forest extended to the Quantocks.

The church of St Mary is one of the most beautiful Perpendicular churches in the county, with a highly decorated 15th century tower. Excavations in recent years reveal that the churchyard was temporarily extended in the 14th century for the burial of plague victims. If the old superstition is accurate, there must have been many a tall, smoking candle flame in those grim days, for this sign is said to portend disaster. Watch your candles carefully in North Petherton, for a spark in the candle's wick is a 'letter from God'.

Today North Petherton, one of the largest villages in Somerset, spreads along a curve in the A38 between Taunton and Bridgwater and consolidates around a close pattern of streets. The busy M5 skirts the village just to the east.

Norton Fitzwarren

'Norton was a market town
When Taunton was a furzy down . . .'

So says the old rhyme, which has its variations all over the south west. It is a proud boast, for Taunton was founded as far back as 710 AD. But above the village of Norton Fitzwarren is an Iron Age fort which was also of importance in Roman times, so perhaps the claim is justified. With the modern expansion of Taunton, there might well be a case for the old adage about joining them if you can't beat them. The ancient earthwork was believed to be the haunt of an enormous serpent who spent most of his time devastating the surrounding countryside and striking terror into innocent folks' hearts. Some people think that this dragon-like creature was the inspiration for the carving on the chancel screen in All Saints Church.

Norton Fitzwarren, which originally stretched along a single, winding village street is now a miscellany of the old and new. It is in the heart of the Vale of Taunton's famous apple growing country, originally a cottage and farmhouse industry where the old wooden cider presses squeezed juice from the apples. Recipes evolved in various ways, for experience showed that almost anything added to the cider gave it extra body. This was literally true, for hunks of meat were often emptied in. Ginger, honey, dates and many other things found their way into the cider, not to mention the occasional horse shoe to increase the iron content, and no doubt bring good fortune. Labourers received firkins of cider as part of their wages, but this tended to be the weak, wrung out remnants of the brew rather than that containing the added refinements. The cider making tradition continues at Taunton Cider Company's factory here.

Norton Fitzwarren grew in importance as a busy railway junction along the London to Exeter route. In March 1862 the branch line from here to Watchet opened and it was extended to Minehead 12 years later. The whole track was laid to the Great Western broad gauge of 7′0¼″ and converted to standard gauge in 1882. The West Somerset Railway Company became part of the Great Western Railway in 1923 and was incorporated into the Western Region of British Railways in 1948. In 1971 the line was closed, but the track was left *in situ*, and the present West Somerset Railway Company operates from Bishops Lydeard and Minehead. Sadly, Norton Fitzwarren had been the scene of two serious railway accidents. The first, in November 1890, involved a head-on collision between a passenger and a goods train when ten people were killed, and the second and more serious accident occurred fifty years later in 1940 when a Penzance express was derailed and twenty-seven lives were lost.

Norton Fitzwarren was the home of the ill-fated hunting squire who celebrated a little too well one New Year's Eve at Langford Budville. He set off for home merrily enough at around midnight, but his horse swerved in terror as they encountered a phantom pack of black hounds on the way. As Somerset folk know well, these are the Devil's hounds, to be treated with tact if one hopes to emerge from such a situation unscathed. Had he been sober, the squire might have been rather more cautious, but as it was he cursed them and lunged out impatiently with his whip. A jagged green flame shot up the stem of the whip scorching the rider and causing the horse to stumble and fall, breaking both of their necks. Thereafter it seems that the ill-fated squire repeats his attempts to complete that homeward journey every New Year's Eve.

Norton St Philip

South of Bath on the A366, today's Norton St Philip is just inside the border which now cuts the old county of Somerset into Avon and Somerset. From about 1230 until the dissolution of the monasteries it belonged to Hinton Priory, and from 1255 until late in the 19th century a 3 day fair was held annually to mark the festival of St Philip and St James. By medieval times it was recognised as the most noteworthy cloth fair in the area, being also the collecting point for Mendip wool. Woollen and linen cloth were sold and the handsome old George Inn was used as an exchange by the cloth merchants.

Norton St Philip, the George Inn

This pleasing and stylish inn is the village showpiece and is considered 'one of the most remarkable medieval inns in England.' It has mullioned and bow windows, much half timbering, a fine porch and a rear courtyard. The inn has a place in history on many counts. Pepys and his household 'dined very well' there for ten shillings in 1668. The Duke of Monmouth made it his base in June 1685 on turning back from Bath. At that time the inn was offering 35 beds and stabling for 90 horses. While he was there he narrowly escaped a would be assassin's bullet, fired through the window.

According to local knowledge, 9 village men were bound to stakes and burnt alive as followers of Monmouth in the campaign of grim retribution which followed his defeat at the Battle of Sedgemoor in 1685. Eight of them had been imprisoned in appalling circumstances at the George for about a year, in the section now known as the Dungeon Bar: the other man who died was an innocent bystander who got swept along with events at the time of the executions.

A path leads across a gently sloping field to the church of St Philip, which dates from the 13th century, but underwent vast alterations by wealthy merchant Jeffrey Flower who designed the rather unorthodox tower. Samuel Pepys admired the music of the 6 bells, which he described as 'mighty tuneable.' He also referred to the 'Fair Maids of Foxcote', Siamese twins joined at the abdomen, who are buried here.

Norton-sub-Hamdon

Norton-sub-Hamdon lies to the west of Montacute and is dominated by Ham Hill, which is capped by an Iron Age fort later used by the Romans and Saxons. This is where the famous warm-toned Ham Hill stone was quarried to provide the stone for building Somerset's most pleasing villages. The hilltop offers a fine vantage point from which to savour these mellow villages set amidst a rolling landscape. The impressive hill can itself be viewed to advantage from points along the A303.

The village, which now increasingly finds itself on the tourist map by virtue of its Country Park, has a mainly 16th century church with a 14th century tower, a 17th century manor house and The Close, with mullioned windows also dating from the 17th century. To the south of the church is an ancient, circular dovecote.

Nunney

The village of Nunney on the eastern flank of the Mendips just to the south west of Frome, was rated 'a perfect village' by Donald Maxwell in his book *Unknown Somerset*, published in 1927. Its moated castle was considered to be 'aesthetically the most impressive castle in Somerset' by Nikolaus Pevsner, the architectural authority. The castle was thought to have been built in 1373 by Sir John de la Mere, who, having arrived home from the French wars laden with booty, obtained permission to fortify and crenelate his manor house. Perhaps with recollections of France to the fore, the construction was based on the Bastille, built to a rectangular plan with 4 boldly rounded corner towers with conical tops and accommodation on 4 floors. It became a Royalist stronghold during the Civil War, but it was eventually taken by Cromwell, who destroyed many of the inner walls to make it useless, as was his custom. A 30 lb cannon ball used in the attack was placed in the 13th century church of All Saints. After the castle had been thus ruined, William Whitchurch built nearby Castle House, now known as Castle Farm.

Nunney's market was licensed by the Crown back in 1260. As the Mendip woollen industry developed, nearby Frome expanded rapidly. Work was farmed out to local towns and villages including Nunney, and master clothiers did the weekly rounds delivering wool and collecting spun yarn. A factory was operating in the village in the last century, but trade died away partly because of the competition from the north with its fast changing technology. Wool used to be washed in the brook near the castle and the church.

The waters of Nunney Brook, which flow down from the Mendips to join the Mells River and then the Frome, were also harnessed to provide power for an outpost of the neighbouring Mells ironworks, which produced high quality agricultural tools.

Today the village with its romantic ruin is much visited by tourists. The island in the moat now functions as a bird sanctuary; a concept undreamed of when the scheme was first envisaged.

Marston Bigot, 1½ miles to the east, is the site of Marston House, built by the Earl of Cork and Orrery around the beginning of the 18th century and extensively remodelled in 1857. It suffered damage when it was used by the army in the war and was later converted into flats.

Nunney Castle

Nynehead

Nynehead is situated to the north of Wellington and was formerly known as Nichehede, Ninehead Flory and Ninehead before becoming Nynehead. At the time of Domesday it was a property of the Bishops of Winchester, and it later came into the possession of the de Fluri and de Wyke families.

The river flows through the attractive grounds of Nynehead Court, which dates mainly from 1675, but was acquired by the Sandfords in about 1600. It was visited by Gainsborough, who painted on the east wall of the church during his stay. The red, sandstone church of All Saints is an unexpected showplace containing a remarkable collection of Italian works of art, including sculptures attributed to Mino de Fiesole, Granacci and Andrea della Robbia and Luca della Robbia.

Oake

The Hillfarrance Brook runs close to the little village of Oake, with the solid, English ring to its name, to the north of Wellington. There are pleasing views across the green, gentle and very English landscape of the Vale of Taunton Deane.

Its red, sandstone church of St Bartholomew has a Tudor pulpit and a 13th century font. Rather unusually in a little church of this type, its south porch is richly embellished with a quatrefoil frieze.

Oakhill

The Mendip village of Oakhill lies to the north of Shepton Mallet and was once famous for its brewery. In the Eastern Mendips the regular supply of good quality springwater was found to be ideal for the brewing of beer and stout, and Oakhill Brewery was the best known of a string of local breweries. It was founded back in 1767 by Jillard & Spencer and was taken over and run by the brothers John and Frederick Spencer in 1882. Most of the houses were built for brewery workers at the end of the last century. Quarry workers from nearby villages sometimes worked the winter months at the brewery.

In 1904 the flourishing company constructed a fine little 2½ feet gauge private railway, which linked the brewery with Binegar

Station on the Somerset and Dorset line, known affectionately as the 'S & D' or 'Slow & Dirty'. Two little saddle tank engines called *Oakhill* and *Mendip* hauled their cargoes of barrels along to Binegar, from where it was distributed to points all over the country. The brewery prospered until the First World War when there were restrictions on the uses of grain. In 1925 there was a bad fire at the brewery which was subsequently taken over and re-sold, with the result that the name has now been lost.

Centuries before achieving recognition with its beer and stout, Oakhill was well known to the Romans, for on the Fosse Way above the village is tree clad Beacon Hill, a Roman landmark for miles around.

At nearby Ashwick, on secondary roads just to the north, is the 19th century Ashwick House, and Ashwick Court dating from around 1700, while at Nettlebridge, just to the east, excavations have unearthed late Neolithic and Early Bronze Age pottery.

Oare

Oare parish, one of the largest in this part of Somerset, has a tiny, scattered population which has always gleaned a livelihood from farming, and was once part of the ancient hunting forest of Exmoor. Life was then very restricted by the forest laws and one parson of 'Ar' was fined 20 shillings for aiding and abetting his son and his servant, who had removed a hind from the forest which had been shot with an archer's arrow.

Situated in a deep valley near the coast, just off the A39 Porlock to Lynmouth road, the village lies hidden from the sea. When the wind is still the silence is broken by the evocative sounds of Oare Water cascading down from Robbers' Bridge towards Badgworthy (pronounce Badgery) Water, recalling the heady romance of R.D. Blackmore's novel *Lorna Doone.* Although John Ridd alluded to 'the little town of Oare', it was never more than a small village.

R. D. Blackmore's grandfather, who was rector here from 1809-1842 used to ride over the moors to preach sermons on alternate Sundays. He absorbed the spirit of the place and its people and influenced the future writer by spinning yarns about his experiences. These seeds were to bear fruit and emerge as *Lorna Doone,* an acclaimed masterpiece. There is a relief portrait in the church commemorating R.D. Blackmore's birth in 1825 and a further plaque on the Malmsbury to Bagworthy track commemorating the centenary of the publication of *Lorna Doone* in 1969.

Oare church is high and remote and is a small, plain stone building with a low tower, somewhat altered since the legendary Lorna stood at the altar as the ring was slipped on her finger, and Carver Doone's shots rang out through the church.

Oare Manor, near the church, was the residence of the late Nicholas Snow, a member of the famly which had held property in the parish for 1,000 years. The Prince of Wales was entertained to tea here when he visited Oare in 1863. Farmer Snow was based on Nicholas Snow, who is buried in the churchyard in Blackmore's book.

Plovers Barrows Farm, the home of the book's hero John Ridd, cannot readily be found, but some say it was at Oareford. At Hoccombe there are ruins of houses thought to have been occupied by the Doones in the 17th century. It is satisfying to link the landscape with literature and in writing *Lorna Doone* R.D. Blackmore captured the multiple spirit of the place and its characters, but it can sometimes be frustrating for those who look for physical evidence of things which live in the book and in the reader's imagination.

Oareford, *see* Oare

Odcombe

This hill crest village to the west of Yeovil, with its variously dated Ham stone houses and cottages and lofty church, is notable for having been the birthplace of 2 sons of former rectors, both of whom made their mark in very differing ways.

Thomas Coryate, born at the rectory in 1577, was an individualist. He was intelligent, whimsical, witty and had a great sense of exploration and adventure. Although educated at Oxford, he failed to gain a degree, but succeeded in being appointed as jester to the Court of James I. At the age of 31 the self styled 'Odcombe Leg Stretcher' set out on a 5 month walking tour of Europe, during the course of which he covered around 2,000 miles. This record-breaking, pedestrian globe-trotter returned to ceremoniously hang up his shoes in the church as an expression of thanks for a safe return, and then set about writing a book about his exploits entitled *'Crudities hastily gobbled up in five month's travel, newly digested in the hungry air of Odcombe'*. Despite his zany exploits he was a scholar and a thinking man, learning much from his experiences and broadening the minds of others. He was responsible for introducing the table fork into our everyday lives, which was a great improvement on sharing communal dishes with other people's dirty fingers. Once when he came upon a gang of armed robbers and could have been in a very difficult situation, he had the presence of mind to whip off his hat and beg *them* for money. Having thus turned the tables he was well equipped for a better-than-usual dinner, bed and breakfast. After 4 years his feet were getting itchy again, and he stood by the market cross to announce to villagers that he would be returning in about 10 years' time. He travelled to Greece, Constantinople, the Middle East, Mesopotamia, Persia and India. On his return journey he was struck down with dysentry in Surat, where he died in 1617. Despite his preoccupation with travel, his home village and Somerset were never far from his thoughts.

The other son of an Odcombe rector, Humphrey Hody, born in 1659, became Regius Professor of Greek at Oxford, wrote learned and occasionally whimsical religious treatises and in his will founded ten exhibitions for the study of Hebrew and Greek at Wadham College.

Old Cleeve

The delightful, mellow village of Old Cleeve is just over a mile from the coast and lies to the south west of Watchet half encompassed by a loop of the West Somerset Railway. Its 15th century church, built on the site of a Saxon church, has many interesting furnishings including a 15th century effigy of an unknown person with a cat at his feet holding a rat in its paw. In the churchyard stands a tall Cross which was battered in Cromwellian times but restored in 1909. There is a tombstone to a blacksmith bearing a traditional inscription relating to his time honoured trade, also found in other parts of the country:

'My Sledge and Hammer lie reclined,
My Billows too have lost their wind;
Me Fire's extinct, my Forge decay'd,
And in the Dust my Body's laid;
My Coal is burnt, my Iron's gone,
My Nails are drove, my Work is done.'

Chapel Cleeve, just north of Old Cleeve is all that remains of a grange of Cleeve Abbey and is now incorporated into a dwelling house. Cleeve Abbey, which is situated to the south of Washford is regarded as the crowning glory of this 'Vallis Florida', (Valley of Flowers). Founded for the Cistercians in 1198 by William de Romara, it bears over the gatehouse a Latin inscription meaning 'This gate shall ever be open to all those who enter honestly'. At the time of the Dissolution, the King's Receiver was so struck by the piety and hospitality of the monks that he pleaded for the place to be spared. However, his pleas were ignored. Today the abbey, which retains its atmosphere of peace and tranquillity, is open to the visiting public.

The seemingly work-a-day name of Washford is probably a derivation of 'Watchet-Ford'. The pleasant village with its thatched cottages and colourful gardens was on the course of the old mineral railway linking the mining areas round Brendon Hill with the port of Watchet (*see* Gupworthy, Luxborough and Roadwater). It is also on the route of the revived West Somerset Railway which runs along the section of coast from Minehead and inland to Bishops Lydeard. Washford is the base for the Somerset & Dorset Railway Museum Trust.

Orchard Portman

Orchard Portman, close to the M5 motorway to the south of Taunton, derives its name from the uniting by marriage of the Portman and Orchard families. The little church of St Michael, set away from other buildings has a Norman north doorway, Perpendicular nave and chancel, and monuments to the Colles family. Orchard House, the ancient manor of the Portman family, was demolished towards the end of the 19th century.

The village, which has fruitful connotations in its name and is dominated by gently rolling green and wooded hills, caught the attention of Thomas Gerard, a local antiquarian. In 1633 he recorded that it 'well brookes the name, for it is seated in a very fertile soyle for fruit; and the whole Countrey thereabouts seems to be orchards, insomuch that all the hedgerows and pasture groundes are full frought with fruite trees of all sorts fittinge to eat and make cider of'.

There are few orchards in the immediate vicinity today, and for many visitors who tread the turf hereabouts, the apple of their eye is their winning horse, for this area now plays host to Taunton Racecourse with stables, polo club and associated activities.

Not far away is Stoke St Mary, beneath Stoke Hill, where folk used to say that a funeral shroud must be warm, for the grave is so cold. At Stoke St Mary, Stoke Court has a two storey porch and early 17th century mullioned windows. The church has a 13th century west tower.

Orchardleigh, *see* Lullington

Othery

Othery, one of the villages of the former island once known as Zoyland, clusters around its church of St Michael and commands fine views across King's Sedge Moor and North Moor. This area offered excellent summer pasture, providing grazing for the flocks of the West Saxon herdsmen after the spring floods had retreated. Othery, Greylake Fosse and Greinton are some of the best places from which to savour the unique spirit and beauty of the area and reflect on its turbulent history.

Otterhampton

This area of flat marsh between Stogursey and the Parrett was a forgotten corner of Somerset, once dotted with windmills. The little village is thought to have gained its name from a Saxon thane and it lies just to the north west of Combwich. Otterhampton is the burial place of an Elizabethan alchemist called Thomas Charnock. He was a remarkable character who travelled around in search of knowledge and developed a particular interest in alchemy. Having been apprenticed to an aged alchemist of Salisbury, he was entrusted with the valuable secret of turning cheap metals into gold by means of the 'philosophy stone' as the old man lay gasping on his deathbed. Following out the complicated 'Midas' technique was to prove somewhat tricky. In 1555, after months of painstaking work, he was just about to achieve a breakthrough when the whole lot exploded in flames. Bitterly disappointed, he patiently started again. Shortly before a triumphant climax there was a commotion outside and banging on his door — and the press gang arrived. The delicately poised experiment was ruined, and in frustration he picked up a hatchet and smashed it all to smithereens. He later married a Somerset heiress and lived in Stockland Bristol and later Combwich. Possibly as a result of married bliss, or perhaps because he no longer needed money, he dropped his experimental alchemistic activities in favour of quietly studying and writing obscure works. One wonders what the medieval mind would have made of nearby Hinkley Point Nuclear Power Station?

Pawlett

The north west slopes of the Poldens descend to the lush pasturelands of the Pawlett Hams, partially encompassed by the enormous meanderings of the shallow Parrett estuary south of Burnham-on-Sea.

The village of Pawlett, locally pronounced 'Pollitt' is clustered around its Norman church on slightly raised ground in a sweep of rich pastureland. There is evidence of Roman and medieval occupation and the ferry was formerly an important link on a busy route much used by pilgrims. Local folk believe that there was a serious accident here in the coaching days, for there were sightings of a phantom coach, complete with driver, guard and a full complement of passengers on the old lane leading to the ferry.

This area of willow-fringed rhines and low pastures has long been recognised for its unique and gentle charms. Back in 1799 Richard Warner observed that 'this part of Somerset exhibits the province of Holland in miniature'. This lush and fertile area is famous for its dairy cattle and has been described as the richest grazing in the country. Water covering it in winter deposits rich silt which creates a particularly strong and succulent growth. Today the growing period can be extended by the use of flood control systems.

Pendomer, *see* **Hardington Mandeville**

Penselwood

The village of Penselwood lies in an area rich in prehistory on the long, wooded ridge separating Somerset from Wiltshire and very close to the Dorset border. It is generally acknowledged to be the site of the battle of Peonnan in 658, which opened up the West Country to the advancing Saxons. Kenwalch's Castle, an Iron Age camp to the north of the village in Castle Wood is named after Cenwealh, the victorious Saxon.

Strategically situated, the place possessed two defensive castles; Bullands Castle and Castle Orchard, Both are very skilfully sited and both are now reduced to grass covered mounds. The origin of Pen Pits, a collection of circular depressions covering several hundred acres is rather obscure. Several colourful theories have been put forward, but it is now generally thought that they are nothing more romantic than excavations for materials to provide grindstones.

The mainly 15th century church of St Michael has a Norman south doorway, and a Norman font. Three of the roof bosses came from Staverdale Priory, an Augustinian establishment founded in 1263, which lies to the north west of the village.

Pilton

About 6 miles to the east of Glastonbury, scattered amongst hills, is Pilton, one of the most delightful villages of East Mendip. Its large and interesting church reflects architectural styles from the time of the Normans.

The impressive 100 ft long tithe barn was once a possession of the abbots of Glastonbury, used to store the crops grown on the estate. Their nearby dovecote supplied meat for the table in lean times and there was a bountiful supply of fish. Sculptured symbols of the four Evangelists adorn the gables of the building, which has a heavily beamed roof. The Manor, which was used as a summer house by the abbots of Glastonbury, bears vestiges of medieval work in some of its windows and on the south side of the turret. It has 16th century mullions and a facade, mostly dating from Georgian times.

This area around Glastonbury is steeped in romantic legends surrounding Joseph of Arimathea and King Arthur. The opportunity to visit Glastonbury, with its Abbey, Rural Life Museum and 15th century Glastonbury Tribunal which contains relics of the lake villages, is one not to be missed.

Pitminster

Known by the melodic name of Pipeminster at the time of Domesday, Pitminster lies at the edge of the Blackdown Hills to the south of Taunton and close to the M5. Because of its situation, it has found itself in the path of generations of invaders crossing the Blackdowns to converge on Taunton. During the Civil War Goring lodged in the village, where trees were hastily felled to act as barricades for holding back the pursuers. Following Monmouth's defeat, fugitives sought refuge in the countryside hereabouts. A double locked wooden coffer containing a horde of French coins probably intended to have been retrieved by the rebel followers was discovered by accident in a local farmhouse. A similar hoard was discovered at nearby Blagdon.

The manor was given to Winchester Cathedral by King Hardicanute. Poundisford Park, to the north of the village, was a Chase of the Bishops of Winchester, who also held Taunton Castle. It was allocated to the Coles family by Henry VII. The lovely Tudor manor house, built in the form of an H, has gabled wings, recessed courts and mullioned windows. In the grounds are a 17th century summerhouse and a building thought to have been the original kitchen. In 1534, when the Chase was divided, Roger Hill was given the lease for what became Poundisford Lodge, built in similar style to the mansion at Poundisford Park, on the site of a former park lodge.

In a landscape dominated by towered churches, it is refreshing to see the west tower of St Andrew and St Mary's topped by a lead and timber spire surmounted by a weather cock. The church contains a number of monuments to the Coles family.

Blagdon Hill, formerly a wild area and animal haunt, may have derived its name from 'blag-don', indicating a 'wolf-hill'.

Porlock

Enclosed to landward by the high terrain of Exmoor, the lovely village of Porlock, with its delightful whitewashed cottages and haphazard, narrow streets enjoys a north facing, seaward aspect. These conditions combine to funnel the warm, moist air upwards, thus encouraging dense, luxuriant growth. This beautiful and spectacular area of hillside vegetation and cascading waters on the shores of Porlock Bay is steeped in romanticism and history and was once a favourite haunt of smugglers.

Porlock's Saxon palace attracted the unwanted attentions of raiders. In 918 the inhabitants warded off the attacks of Danish pirates and in 1052 Harold Godwinsson, who set sail from Ireland with 9 ships on an expedition to plunder and murder, attacked the place and set it ablaze.

The church with its short, shingled tower and spire was said to have been truncated in a storm of 1700. It was dedicated to St Dubricius, reputed to have officiated at the wedding of King Arthur and Queen Guinevere. The story goes that this Celtic saint so loved Porlock that he settled here and lived to the extremely ripe old age of 150 years.

Porlock has connections with the poets Southey and Coleridge. A chimney corner of the lovely old Ship Inn is devoted to the memory of Southey who sought refuge here in a storm. He was so entranced with the beauty of the area that he composed a sonnet by the alehouse fire, inspired by the fair and lovely Vale of Porlock. He also recorded that 'this place is called in the neighbourhood "the End of the World". All beyond is inaccessible to carriage or even cart. A sort of sledge is used by the country people, resting upon two poles like cart shafts'. This transporter was known as a 'trackamuck' in those days.

Samuel Taylor Coleridge, poet and philosopher, who lived for a short period at nearby Nether Stowey, rested at a farm near Porlock during one of his solitary moorland walks across Exmoor. He fell into a deep sleep after taking drugs and awoke with a vision of the poem which was to become *Kubla Khan.* He began writing straight away while it was fresh in his mind, but as he was in full flow he was disturbed by a visitor from Porlock. When he returned to his writing, the spell was broken and he was unable to finish the poem, which remains uncompleted.

Porlock Hill, with its gradient of 1 in 4 has always been a test for vehicles and their drivers, and can be a ruthless test of one's brakes and skill in hill starts. It was first attempted by motor car in 1900 in response to a bet. The scene of quite a number of mishaps, ancient and modern, it is believed to have witnessed a calamity in the coaching days when a coach and four ran out of control down the hill with fatal consequences for all concerned. The ghostly, grey horses with their ill-fated passengers are said to haunt the hill.

The road from Porlock descends through West Porlock with its picturesque, whitewashed cottages to Porlock Weir, the ancient port of Porlock, with its delightful harbour, cottages and buildings of great character and charm, riding stables and sailing club. At Eastertide it was customary for folk to decorate their houses with certain spring flowers, according to tradition, and evergreen branches were placed over the front doors in symbolic style.

Porlock Bay, described by the early historian Leland as 'a meatly good rode for shippes' played an important part in Exmoor's history, the sea route providing the most convenient way in and out of the area. Porlock was known at the time of Domesday as 'Portloc', meaning an enclosed harbour. Once a thriving trading port and market town, Porlock finds itself busy these days as a visitors' showpiece. Dovery Court, at the entrance to the village and once the Dower House attached the manor of Porlock, now functions as an Information Centre for modern day travellers. There are some spectacular walks along the coast and a superb scenic drive to Lynmouth with the sea on one side and moorland on the other.

Porlock Harbour

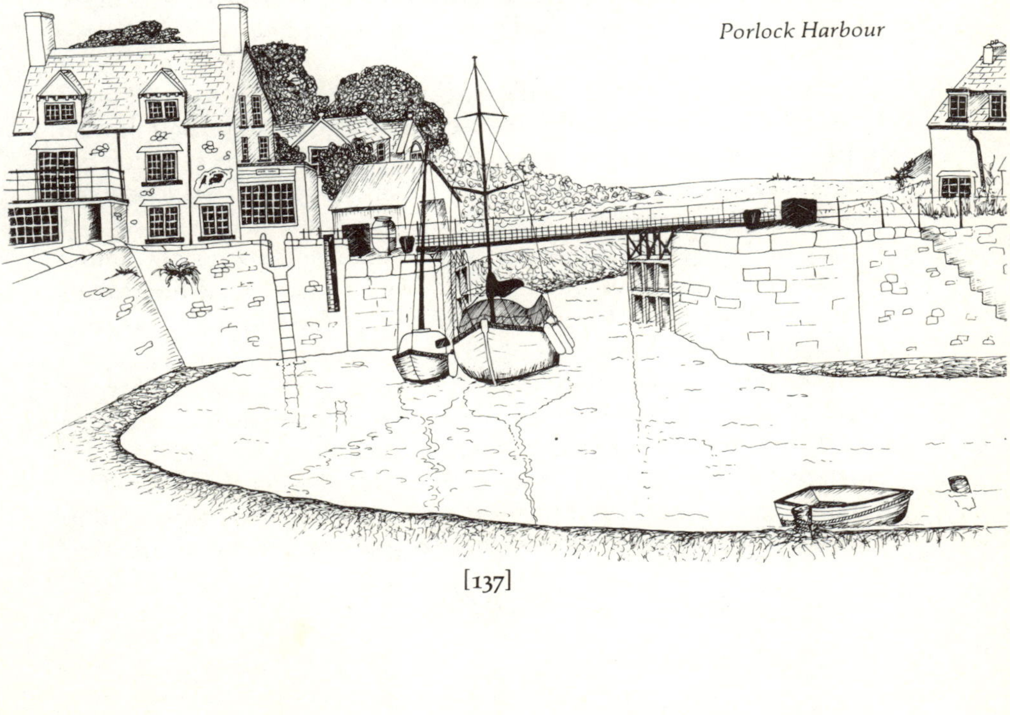

Poundisford, *see* Pitminster

Priddy

High on the broad windswept plateau of the Mendips is the ancient lead settlement of Priddy, lying in its shallow hollow about 800 feet above sea level. 'Prid' is a Celtish word meaning high; this is the highest village in Somerset and one of the highest in England. It lies in an area extremely rich in prehistoric remains. Priddy Nine Barrows, Priddy Stone Circles and Ashen Hill Barrow are to the north east of the village, with a long barrow to the west and tumuli all around. The course of a Roman road ran just to the east. The source of the River Axe rises nearby, to disappear quickly into an underground cave or 'swallet'. Open cast lead mining activities have left 'gruffy' ground to the east of the village. The mining areas of Mendip were once divided into 4 sections, each of which was under the control of a Lord Royal (*see* Charterhouse).

The lovely legend of Priddy told of a rich metal merchant called Joseph of Arimathea whose trade brought him to the port of Watchet. Sometimes the young Jesus would accompany him. The boy Jesus is said to have walked the Quantocks to Bridgwater, crossed to the foot of Mendip by punt to make his way through the lanes to Priddy where he talked to the miners. This story is so deep-rooted that a local saying used to back up a point went 'and that's as sure as Christ came to Priddy!'

In the village is an old hurdle stack, a symbol of the ancient wool trade which also ensures the right of local folk to hold their annual market on the Green. It is said that the annual Sheep Fair, which has been functioning for over 600 years was diverted to Priddy when Wells was devastated with the plague. This may have been so, but Priddy had long been a place of importance in its own right, and a network of lanes converged here. Priddy Fair has the distinction of being the first place for traders to have used unified measures. Primarily a Sheep Market, it widened its scope to include cattle and horse dealing, and in the 18th and 19th centuries it catered for the needs of the local miners. Folk who came to the market liked to be entertained and there would be contests including cheese rolling and boisterous prize fights — then essential for a successful fair. This annual, August event, looked forward to all year and savoured in retrospect, was so much an established part of the way of life that they measured the seasons by it. The first wet day after the excitement of the fair was counted as 'the first rain of winter'. These days there are stalls and stands displaying and selling agricultural goods, clothing and other tempting wares with catering vans selling snacks and ice creams to the crowds.

Ebbor Gorge, just to the south, is owned by the National Trust and run as a nature reserve.

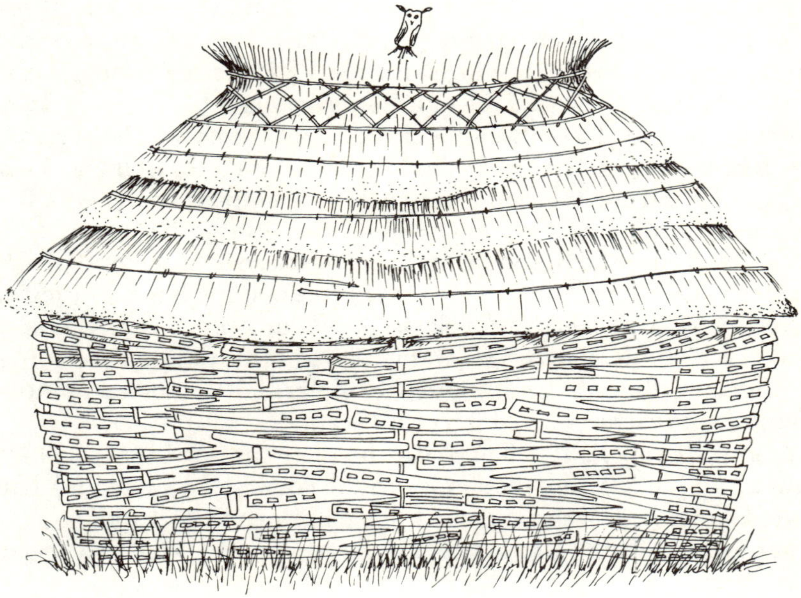

Priddy, hurdle stack

Puritan, *see* **Cossington**

Purtington, *see* **Cudworth**

Queen Camel

In the 1540's the historian Leland who rode through the village on a journey from South Cadbury to Ilchester recorded that 'al this way the pastures and feeldes be much enclosed with heggerowes of elmes'.

Situated in the shelter of Camel Hill, this enchantingly named place with its pleasing architecture derived its 'Cam' connection from being close to Cadbury Castle which many believe to have been King Arthur's Camelot. It was also the property of queens, and was given as a dowry in 1019 by Godwyn, Earl of Essex, to his wife Gytha, mother of the Saxon King Harold. Following the Battle of Hastings, William the Conqueror granted the manor to his Queen Matilda.

In 1555 the manor of Queen Camel was transferred by the Crown to Sir Walter Mildmay, MP, in exchange for an estate in Norfolk. Hazelgrove House, set in beautiful parkland on the other side of the river adjacent to the village of Sparkford is the old house of the Mildmays. Although retaining some of its Elizabethan work, it was remodelled into an exact copy of a Genoese palace by Carew Hervey Mildmay in 1720. The entrance arch alongside the A303 is the gateway brought here from the unfinished house of Lord Stawell (*see* Low Ham). Hazelgrove House is now used as a preparatory school for Bruton School.

The church of St Barnabas, which is reckoned to be one of the most beautiful Perpendicular churches in the county, has a 4 storeyed tower containing 6 bells and a clock. A Welshman, Thomas Charles, who was a curate here in 1778 and who had some difficulty in being accepted by the villagers, moved to Bala and became a notable Methodist preacher in the land of his birth.

A spring rising in the village near the river has medicinal qualities with a sulphurous content similar to the waters of Harrogate. The River Cam flows on through the village of West Camel and under a delightful old packhorse bridge before joining the River Yeo near Yeovilton.

Raleigh's Cross, *see* Luxborough

Redlynch

Back in 1569 the little village of Redlynch, just to the south east of Bruton, had a population of around 40 people, including 10 able bodied men over the age of 16. Its church was one of 5 local churches of the Priory of Augustinian Canons, founded at Bruton in 1142. However, Redlynch, in common with Cricket St Thomas, was to be swept away so that Redlynch Park could be extended. Where once there was a village, a beautifully landscaped park now sweeps southwards to a lake surrounded by trees.

Redlynch Park, seat of the Earls of Ilchester, was originally the property of the ancient Draycott family. In the 15th century an heiress married into the Fitzjames family. Richard Fitzjames, a Bishop of London who did much for the building of St Paul's and the Palace at Fulham, was born here. The house was built in 1673 by Sir Stephen Fox, father of the first Earl of Ilchester and the first Lord Holland. It was Sir Stephen and not Nell Gwyn who actually influenced Charles II in the founding of Chelsea Hospital. The mansion at Redlynch was enlarged in the 18th century, but it was badly damaged by fire.

Today just a few estate cottages remain along the main road.

Roadwater

Two streams rise in the Brendon Hills to converge in the pleasant little village of Roadwater and become the Washford River. An evocative sound around these parts is that of fast flowing water.

The old mineral railway from Brendon Hill down to the port of Watchet passed through the village (*see* Gupworthy and Luxborough). Most signs of the railway have disappeared and the track from Roadwater to Comberow has been made into a road. Roadwater's station has become a bungalow and various other industrial buildings have now been adapted for other uses.

There is a Holy Well nearby, in the garden of an old cottage which was formerly a chapel dedicated to St Pancras.

Up through the steep and beautiful area of woodlands and hill streams is the lonely little village at Treborough, with its tiny 19th century church which has a 15th century font. Higher still on Treborough Common to the south is a Bronze Age barrow.

Rode

The tranquil valley of the Frome was formerly busy with activities relating to the cloth industry. Between Woolverton and Rode, the fine 3 arched packhorse bridge of Scutt's Bridge carried horses laden with packs of wool or rolls of cloth on their way over the borders and into Wiltshire. Upstream, a single span bridge crosses a diverted mill stream which formerly supplied Scuttsbridge Mill, now demolished.

According to local tradition, Charles Stuart, who came through the village after his defeat at the Battle of Worcester, surveyed the surrounding countryside from the embattled tower of St Laurence's Church.

Christ Church at Rode Hill to the north of the village was built by the Archbishop Daubeny in 1824. Rode Hill House was the scene of a notorious murder in 1860 when Constance Kent, who lived in apparent harmony with her father, stepmother and stepbrother, murdered her 3 year old stepbrother and hid his mutilated body. This was discovered just a few hours later and although it was obvious that someone in the house was responsible for the murder, it had been planned so cleverly that no one knew who the villain actually was until Constance Kent made a confession 5 years later. She was tried at Salisbury, sentenced to death, but ended up serving 20 years at Portland penitentiary. After returning briefly to the scene of her crime she disappeared into obscurity.

Lying to the east of the village, the imaginatively named Devil's Bed and Bolster is a long barrow scattered with stones, which has never been excavated.

Rode, the packhorse bridge

Rodney Stoke

Rodney Stoke, a pretty village to the north west of Wells, enjoys a beautiful setting beneath the wooded slopes of the high Mendip plateau. Originally named 'Stoke', it acquired the additional name of 'Giffard' when it came into the possession of the Giffard family at the time of King John. Having passed by marriage into the Rodney family, the 'Giffard' was shelved and 'Rodney' took its place. The church of St Leonard has numerous monuments to the Rodney family.

To the north of the church is Manor Farm House, which has a small Elizabethan gatehouse or summerhouse incorporated in its farm buildings. In medieval times goats were kept in this area of the Mendips.

Draycott, just to the north, offers fine views and strawberries. Its mainly 19th century church has some 13th century work and a pretty wrought iron screen.

Roebuck, *see* Stogumber

Rowberrow

The old mining village of Rowberrow is situated high on the bleak and windy Mendip plateau in an area rich in prehistoric remains and caverns. Rowberrow Camp, measuring 200 ft square, may have been a Roman marching camp and evidence of old field systems are discernible on Dolebury Warren. Rowberrow Cavern is one of the caves of Burrington Combe, which is a smaller version of Cheddar Gorge.

Rowberrow's picturesque little church of St Michael lies apart from the village almost on the line of Somerset's border with the newly created county of Avon. From the churchyard there are fine views across Dolebury and between Rowberrow and Shipham there are long vistas across the Bristol Channel.

The village, together with neighbouring Shipham, was of great importance in the 18th century for the production of calamine ore, a vital ingredient used in the brass and zinc industries of Bristol. In those days the mining communities were notoriously tough and lawless. Despite this Hannah More, born in 1755, with her sister Martha, daughters of a Bristol schoolmaster set about improving the lot of the downtrodden mining folk. She forged ahead with establishing a school here and in the neighbouring villages as well as other philanthropic, practical gestures, and she wrote prolific religious tracts which sold widely. Through her writings we gain insight into their lives at that time.

Although mining for calamine ore remained profitable for longer than lead mining, the industry was in decline by the middle of the 19th century, mostly as the result of overseas competition. There were a number of abortive attempts to revive it over the next 50 years.

Rudge, *see* **Beckington**

St Audries, *see* **West Quantoxhead**

Sampford Arundel

Sampford Arundel, to the south west of Wellington and close to the Devon border, lies between the main Paddington to Penzance railway, the M5 and a tributary of the River Tone. Its name stems from Sand-ford a crossing over the little waterway, and Arundel, after Roger Arundel, who was given the manor after the Norman Conquest. In the 18th century it passed to the Baker family and it came into the possession of Thomas Ware the following century.

The church of the Holy Cross, with its 13th century tower, has an unusual sculpture of hands holding a heart, recalling a line from the hymn 'Now Thank We All Our God . . . with hearts and hands and voices . . .' Retaining a heavenly theme, Holywell Lake to the north of the village and on the other side of the railway is on the site of a holy well. Strangely, the place has an inn but no church. Rather less than heavenly was the old custom of cudgel-fighting and bull baiting practised outside the inn.

Seavington St Mary

The name 'Seavington' probably alludes to its early situation as a place of seven settlements surrounded by Easterdown Hill to the south, Boxstone to the north and west and a large open area to the north east. A quarry with its limekiln was situated on the northern side of Easterdown Hill. The area was well known to the Romans and a villa has been discovered between here and Dinnington, with the Fosse Way nearby. In coaching days the old Travellers' Rest in Muckleditch Lane on the Taunton road provided a welcome haven.

Among the ancient and attractive names for furlongs, fields and meadows are Pitfurlong, Middle furlong, Stone furlong, Merfield, Rye field, Westfield, Higher fields, Lower fields, Upton mead and South mead, which incorporate directional or other means of identification. Hurcott and Upton farm houses are thought to date from the 17th century and the present rectory was also a farm house until 1890.

Agriculture was always the mainstay. They kept sheep and cattle and grew wheat, oats, barley, beans, potatoes, peas, clover, flax and hemp. Flax and hemp and wool were much in demand from neighbouring towns for the weaving and cloth trade; flax and hemp for the manufacture of sailcloth. A hundred years ago women and girls carried out glovemaking in their homes, but by the beginning of this century many of them had found employment at the collar factory in Ilminster.

The church of St Mary, constructed of rubble with ashlar dressings, has a 13th century chancel and nave, with a later tower. In 1577 the peace of respectable churchgoers was affronted by a woman 'suspected to be a sorcerer'.

The little village of Whitelackington, to the west, has a church with a 15th century tower and a 16th century manor house next to it. At nearby Hurcott are the remains of a defensive earthwork.

Seavington St Michael

Seavington St Michael lies just east of Seavington St Mary with the old Water Street, Flower Tanner's Lane and Frogmary Lane serving as parish boundary lines. The strange name 'Frogmary' is derived from 'Froggelmere'. Two early routes pass through the parish, and today the village finds itself on the busy A303.

The manor, which once belonged to Glastonbury Abbey, was surrendered to the Crown at the time of the dissolution of the monasteries and given to Winchester College — who sold their holding in 1932. Buckrell's Farm and Orchard Close Farm date from the 17th century, as does Swan Thatch, which was the village bakery before becoming a post office. In the 1800's there were two shops in the village as well as a bakers, a blacksmiths and two inns — the Bell and the Volunteer.

Agriculture was the main occupation. Pigs and sheep were reared and hay, clover, peas, beans, potatoes, barley and wheat were produced. By the end of the 18th century 'a deal' of flax was being grown to supply the local towns engaged in textile production. Enough timber was grown to meet local requirements, most of it oak, ash and elm.

In days of yore the village pond, popularly referred to in the 17th century as the 'horse pond', graced an area alongside the village street. The importance of ponds from the ecological and aesthetic points of view has now been recognised, but there has always been a tendency to take liberties with ponds, and to exploit them for any convenient use. Apart from its obvious connection with horses, this pond was used for retting flax and washing wool before suffering the ultimate indignity of being filled in. The area now serves as a car park.

At the beginning of the 19th century there were two day schools and a Sunday school. The church school, designed to accommodate a hundred children suffered from falling rolls; a situation which was temporarily boosted with an influx of evacuees in 1944 when children were billeted with local families and at the rectory. The school closed in 1968 and the building converted for use as a private residence.

Selworthy

The village of Selworthy is contained within the National Trust's holdings on Exmoor and is acknowledged to be one of the loveliest villages in England, with its well tended whitewashed thatched cottages charmingly set around a green.

The 15th century church, a handsome Perpendicular structure with a square, embattled west tower possesses one of Somerset's most interesting wagon roofs, richly decorated with angels, bosses, shields and symbols. Its south aisle has been described as 'one of the greatest treasures of English architecture'. Just south of the church is a 15th century stone tithe barn and a 16th century cross.

Holnicote House, which has burnt down three times since the end of the 18th century, was the second home of the Aclands of Killerton. Most of the estate was given over to the National Trust in 1944 by Sir Richard Dyke Acland and the house is now used as a holiday centre.

The village lies in the shelter of Selworthy Beacon, which rises to 1,014 feet above sea level. Near the Beacon and overlooking Selworthy Combe is the circular Bury Camp, 200 feet in diameter. The surrounding area is rich in prehistoric evidence. Selworthy lies in an area of exceptionally beautiful countryside, much of it of great scientific significance. Paths through Selworthy woods lead through sections of oak, chestnut, Scots pine and silver fir planted around 1815 by Sir Thomas Dyke Acland.

Tivington's Chapel of St Leonard, dating from the early part of the 15th century is now joined to a thatched cottage of a later date.

Selworthy

Shapwick

Shapwick is one of a string of villages along the gentle northern slopes of the Polden Hills which bisect the flatlands of Somerset. It was once a stopover point for pilgrims on their way to and from Glastonbury Abbey. Numbered among the pilgrims who sought shelter here were St Indractus and his sister, returning to Ireland after a pilgrimage to Rome. Having halted to pay homage at St Patrick's tomb at Glastonbury, they were spotted by servants of King Ina who mistook their brass topped staffs for rods of gold, and their sacks of seeds to be planted in Ireland for bags of booty. They were followed and murdered at Shapwick and their bodies were thrown into a pit. It is said that a heavenly light shone over the pit for 3 days and 3 nights, and when the king learned of the atrocity he had them buried at Glastonbury. Today, a light is seen to appear around that spot to signify an evil deed.

In common with the other villages along this side of the Poldens, Shapwick had its holy well which was rather better known than the others. The water springs from the clays of the Lower Lias and contains mineral salts and sulphuretted hydrogen similar to the therapeutic waters of Harrogate. The waters were exploited around the beginning of the last century when a rather Spartan bath house was erected for the benefit of the visiting sick. However, today's potential pilgrims seeking a cure will look in vain for the bath house, which has been demolished, and the spring, which has been diverted.

The 14th century church has a fine timbered roof and mural tablets to the Bull and Strangways families. Shapwick House was built by Judge Rolles, who had been relieved of office by Cromwell, on the site of the old court house of Abbot John de Taunton. Constructed in the 17th century and altered in the following century, it retains much of its original work. The manor house is gabled and has a 2 storeyed porch. Shapwick has the rare distinction of possessing two ancient icehouses. One is in Icehouse Copse and the other, which is older and thought to be of Norman origin, is at Shapwick House. Icehouses were built penetrating into the ground, stacked with ice in winter, and filled with summer produce in the hope that this would keep in good condition for use the following winter.

A rail link from Highbridge to Glastonbury formerly crossed Shapwick Heath and provided the ideal way to view the turbary. The heath has yielded some fascinating Romano-British finds during the course of peat extraction. The peat industry, which originally provided fuel, has recently enjoyed a revival to cater for a growing horticultural demand. The emphasis has shifted, but the traditional language and methods have remained the same.

Rough, damp, dark, scrubby heathland, where bog myrtle, wild iris, marsh marigold and other varieties geared to our rapidly disappearing wetlands grow is a much valued habitat, and the Nature Conservancy has a reserve at Shapwick Heath. Apart from the botanical interest it provides a breeding ground for many birds including the willow tit, nightjar and nightingale.

Shepton Beauchamp

The riches of Somerset originated in its soil and Shepton Beauchamp, to the north east of Ilminster, is one of the few places where the early cultivation strips and furlongs can still be seen. Back in the 14th century it was customary for a free tenant to be chosen as the hayward, and he would supervise the mowing of the grass and the stacking of the hay, wearing white gloves and carrying a white staff.

Fossil rich rocks discovered in the area in the last century created excitement, and an 1856 guidebook enthused about: 'abundant remains of fossils, saurians, fish crustaceans and insects . . . remarkable for their fine preservation', and pointed out that 'an excellent selection can be seen at Shepton Beauchamp. The insects have been discovered in all stages of growth from the caterpillar to the fly, and beetles so perfect that they seem to be staring at you, their eyes being well defined in the stone'.

The parish of Shepton Beauchamp had a reputation for being highly populated, having once been described as a 'curious place, much over populated, being nearly a person to an acre' — a statistic which might well be the envy of many by today's standards.

Village folk have tended to be gregarious and have always demonstrated how to enjoy themselves. The medieval market and fair was held in the village, probably at the Shambles, and the traditional Shepton Play was an occasion for merrymaking and fun, when cider was given away in the streets. A fife and drum band was formed in 1873, and amongst the inns were the Duke of York, the New Inn and the Red Lion, later known as the George Inn. A Friendly Society founded in 1802 and re-founded in 1847 continued meeting until just before the Second World War. Just behind the New Inn, which closed in 1960, is an old 'fives' wall with curved parapet and ball finials. In 1602 there was a bowling green in the village. Two old country songs collected here by Cecil Sharp in 1905 were published by him.

One 19th century rector saw wickedness in the merrymaking and set about the task of sobering down his flock, although he had to admit defeat when it came to founding a temperance society. His daughter, Julia Coles, played an important role in village life, carrying out welfare and social work. The old rectory served as a home for young girls employed in laundry and housework, and was rather grimly renamed St Michael's Home & Penitentiary. St Gabriel's Cottage in North Street was to house teachers and for training girls in domestic service.

A wide variety of occupations were pursued in the village apart from the usual farming and glove making. These included the making of parchment, baskets, brushes, straw bonnets, skirts, collars, mantuas and biscuits. There were barbers, mercers, drapers, millers, bakers, tobacconists and weavers, and it is known that there were shops in the village in 1645, reaching a peak of nine shops in 1861. Despite such prosperity, many people from the village emigrated in the 18th and 19th century during a period of agricultural turmoil for the labouring classes.

Shipham

Today farming and quarrying are the mainstay of Shipham, which lies peacefully in the western Mendips, just south of Somerset's border with Avon. It is hard to believe that the former mining inhabitants had a reputation for being tough and disorderly. Back in the late 18th century they were described as 'savage and depraved . . . brutal in their natures and ferocious in their manners'. The sisters Hannah and Martha More who made these observations did much to improve the social conditions of the mining families (*see* Rowberrow). They also pointed out that constables were reluctant to get on the wrong side of the lawless Shipham men for fear of disappearing for ever down one of the pits.

Shipham, together with neighbouring Rowberrow, was important for the mining of calamine which thrived from the mid 16th century to the mid 19th century and supplied a ready market in Bristol. Today the grassy hummocks or 'gruffy ground' and the Miners Arms are reminders of a gruelling way of life which has passed.

The surrounding area is rich in prehistoric remains, and the site of a Roman village lies to the north west of Shipham. Nearby is the intriguingly named Wimblestone, an irregularly shaped, weatherbeaten block of stone about 5½ feet high. No one can be certain of its origin, but some folk reckon they are aware of its habits. The stone, which some believe guards a treasure, is said to dance nimbly around the field when there is a full moon on Midsummer Night.

Simonsbath

The high country around Simonsbath, which was formerly part of the old Royal Forest of Exmoor, has undergone considerable changes over the centuries. John Leland described it in the mid 16th century as being 'all by forest, baren and morisch ground, wher ys store and breading of yonge catelle, but little or no corne or habitation'. A century later it was recorded as being 'a solitarie place'. In the mid 17th century James Boevey, a London merchant, acquired the Forest, enclosed and cultivated the land and built himself a fine mansion. But the difficulties of taming the terrain and quarrels with his neighbours defeated his objectives.

In 1815 the upland waste of Exmoor was enclosed by Parliamentary Act. It was purchased by John Knight, a Worcestershire Iron Master who enjoyed the challenge of transforming an unproductive area into an agricultural one. Shepherds and ploughmen were accommodated in bothies in Simonsbath, roads were built and a number of farms were created. Through his work the Parish of Exmoor evolved. The place which had consisted of a solitary farmstead with a family of 5 in 1820 had become a village with a population of 339 by 1871. Cottages, a church, a school, an inn and a Post Office were built. In the 1850s an Iron Master from South Wales, interested in the local iron deposits around Simonsbath began mining and work started on a mineral railway from here to Porlock. However, the project fizzled out.

Attitudes to our environment have changed greatly since those efforts to tame the moors. Today the moorland village of Simonsbath, attractively situated in a well wooded combe with its characteristic buildings flanking the green is a popular tourist centre for Exmoor. It is particularly appreciated as a haven for walkers and those who love wild, unspoilt countryside.

'Simonsbath' is an intriguing name. Some people think that it was connected with Sigmund, the local slayer of dragons. Others think that it is connected with the naming of Symon's Pool, just above the bridge over the River Barle, which got its name from an old rogue called Simon. It seems that ordinary, decent folk so feared the outlaw that they arranged for a saint to be found who might point out to him the error of his ways. A Cornish saint was duly discovered who achieved remarkable success very quickly. Thinking it fitting for such a dastardly sinner to be baptised in a particularly deep pool on an extremely cold day, he was baptised here as a prelude to further baptisms in Cornwall.

South Cadbury

South Cadbury, between Castle Cary and Sherborne, is a little village of leafy, secluded charm lying in a valley and dominated by Cadbury Camp — one of the West Country's best known archaeological sites. Cadbury Castle has long been a strong contender as the Camelot of Arthurian legend. Modern excavation has revealed evidence of successive periods of occupation from early Neolithic times (about 4,000 years BC). Its high, flat plateau with a circumference of nearly a mile has 4 sets of grassy ramparts. From the summit there are magnificent views of the surrounding countryside. In recent years the 'Cadbury dig', which attracts many young volunteers, has become familiar to enthusiasts and TV viewers. Interesting discoveries include weapons, coins, pottery and trinkets.

There are 2 wells on Cadbury encampment known as Arthur's Well and Queen Anne's Well. King Arthur's hounds are said to drink thirstily at his well before following their master on his ghostly rides along the old track towards Glastonbury known as Arthur's Hunting Causeway. Pins dropped into Queen Anne's Well before sunrise foretell one's luck in the marital stakes. A pin aligning with another gives promise of nuptials to come.

It is not surprising that a romantic and mysterious site such as Cadbury attracts colourful myths and legends. The hill, which early folk thought had to be hollow, was believed to be a fairy refuge where they stored their pots of gold. It is said that the fairy folk were frightened away by the sound of the church bells, fleeing in such haste that they left their gold behind them. However they took the sensible precaution of casting a protective spell over it, for the treasure sinks deeper into the hill every time anyone attempts to recover it. King Arthur and his knights (who presumably took over vacant possession) are reputed to sleep in a deep cavern in the hill, emerging occasionally for hectic moonlit rides around the ramparts on silver shod horses. Centuries ago a silver horseshoe was found after just such a frolic.

Sutton Montis, prettily situated to the south of Cadbury camp has a Norman church with a 13th century tower, a 15th century font and a canopied pulpit. Among the attractive and interesting buildings are Abbey House, to the west of the church and the 17th century Parsonage Farm.

South Petherton

Ina, King of Wessex, who devoted himself to enlarging his kingdom as well as to religion and law, had a favourite residence at South Petherton, with the probable site later becoming known as 'Ina's Palace'. The small town was also the resting place of Sir Giles Daubeney, descendant of William the Conqueror's standard bearer who was one time Lord of the Manor, as well as a number of theologians. South Petherton's church is regarded as being one of the most beautiful perpendicular churches in the county.

The little town to the north east of Ilminster, which lies to the centre of a group of hamlets and is connected to them rather like a hub and spokes of a wheel, traditionally served their needs. An ancient route, thought to pre-date the nearby Fosse Way, passes to the south of the town and became incorporated in the 18th century coaching route. There was once a watch house on Petherton Bridge.

An early bridge over the Parrett was referred to at the start of the 13th century as the 'old bridge'. This point of crossing has assumed strategic importance in times of strife, particularly during the Civil War, and it has been repaired at various times throughout history. A modern structure now takes the strain of dual carriageway traffic over the Parrett.

A market house and cross occupied the centre of the medieval town, which originally had a 'Cheap Street' in close proximity. A lock-up which formerly occupied a site near the church gate was replaced with another incorporated inside the Market House. The

Bell Inn, dating from 1622 was rebuilt in 1925, and the 18th century Norris House was named after the doctor and historian who jointly edited *Somerset and Dorset Notes And Queries 1888-90*.

There were at various times a large number of inns around the town and parish with some particularly attractive names, including The George, The Rose & Crown, The Three Cups, The Castle, White Horse, Wheatsheaf, King's Arms, Plough, the Bunch of Grapes and The Running Footman. Present day residents can also draw from a fine cultural tradition encompassing the arts and sciences as well as literary and other topics.

Sparkford, *see* Queen Camel

Spaxton

On the edge of the Quantock Hills and to the west of Bridgwater, the village of Spaxton achieved notoriety in the middle of the last century by the strange goings on of a religious sect which housed themselves here behind high walls in 'The Abode of Love'. These Agapemonites were led by H.J. Prince, a former curate of the neighbouring village of Charlinch, and the mostly female followers tended to be rich and plain, or poor but comely. They gave over all their wealth on joining the sect and addressed their leader, who claimed to be immortal, as 'Beloved'. Although their faith must have been somewhat shaken when he died — in the manner of ordinary mortals — in 1899, the 'New Messiah', the Rev J.H. Smyth Pigott filled the breach successfully. Children resulting from 'divine love' were given fancy names such as Glory, Power and Hallelujah. However, these earthly beings resulted in Smyth Pigott being deprived of his Holy Orders. The villagers, who must have wondered what went on behind those high walls, were very tolerant of the eccentrics in their midst.

The village with its manor house and ancient churchyard cross has an interesting church bearing witness to the area's great woollen trade of the past. It retains some 13th century work and has carvings dated 1536 and 1561.

Nearby Charlinch, enjoys a pleasing setting and commands magnificent views of the Quantocks and across the Severn Estuary to the mountains of Wales.

Don't be so tactless as to ask anyone their age around these parts, for superstition would have you believe that every time you tell your age a year is knocked off your allotted time.

Standerwick, *see* **Beckington**

Staple Fitzpaine

This unspoilt village with its well proportioned stone cottages is set in delightful wooded countryside beneath a ridge of the Blackdown Hills. Its church of St Peter, which has one of the most beautiful towers in Somerset, has a Norman south door, comical gargoyles and a screen to the vestry which came from the old church at neighbouring Bickenhall. The impressive manor house and associated buildings grace the area near the church. The pleasing almshouses endowed in 1643 were restored in 1970. The Greyhound Inn is a favourite local haunt.

The village was previously known as Staple Brieves. The name 'Staple' is thought to have been derived from the Old English 'stapol', indicating a pillar or post, which may refer to the Sarcen stone. This is an ancient stone of a different nature from that found locally, which according to mythology was tossed over from Castle Neroche. It is said to bleed if pricked at certain times of the year. Other such stones are found around the Blackdowns. The second part of the name was changed to 'Fitzpaine' when the Fitzpaine family came on the scene at the time of Edward III. The estate passed to the Portman family, and it was later broken up with the fine woodlands being leased to the Forestry Commission. Staple Fitzpaine is in a particularly enchanting setting amongst what remains of the old medieval forest of Neroche. There are some delightful woodland walks (*see* Buckland St Mary).

Bickenhall, a hamlet just east of Staple Fitzpaine retains romantic echoes of the past in its evocatively named Brandy Bridge and Bottle Bridge. Its church of St Paul was constructed in 1849.

Stapley, *see* **Churchstanton**

Stawell

Stawell, on the southern side of the Polden Hills, has a church with an unfinished tower sealed off with a gable; and therein hangs a tale. The parish of Stawell was in dispute with the sister parishes of Chilton, Catcott, Edington, Greinton, Sutton Mallet and Moorlinch as to which of them should be the principal parish to qualify for receiving the legacy of a fine set of bells. The Lord Abbot who was called in decreed that the gift should go to the first parish to notch up 3 births and 3 deaths. As though predestined to receive such an appealing gift, Stawell got off to a good start with 3 births and 2 deaths. Paying no regard to the proverb about counting chickens before they were hatched, they embarked with great enthusiasm on the building of a tower to house the bells. Before a third inhabitant of Stawell obliged them by dying, Moorlinch pipped them at the post and became the proud recipient of the bells.

The village also has the distinction of being the refuge of the Poldens' own highwayman, a gentleman named Pocock, who was something of a folk hero with a certain equestrian flair and style, and who lived in a cavern. For him, disregarding law and order was not merely a challenge — more of an art. He was adept at covering his tracks and confusing his would-be captors and was credited with ability to swivel the shoes of his horse, thus leading his pursuers fruitlessly to places he had just left. A ballard ran thus:

> 'Run, my boys run, the moon shines bright,
> Pocock's in his cave his purse is light;
> But, when the night is murky and dark,
> He's off with his steed, blithe as a lark.'

A grotto named Pocock's Cell was built in his memory, near Ford Mill.

Stoford, *see* Ash Priors

Stogumber

This large, attractive village which lies in the Brendon foothills amidst rolling farmland took its name from a Norman lord. The picturesque and diverse cottages are dominated by the 14th century church of St Mary which found its way into the history books when a heavenly cannon ball put a halt to Elizabeth Sydenham's marriage. She had been betrothed to Sir Francis Drake, but was going ahead with plans to marry another as Sir Francis had been so long away (*see* Monksilver). In the manner of all the best romantic stories he returned soon afterwards to claim his rightful bride. Some 17th century almshouses grace the main street to the south west of the church.

The wealthy and influential Sydenham family lived in the fine house of nearby Combe Sydenham, and the ghostly cavalier Sir George Sydenham still rides the lanes on certain nights. A phantom pack of hounds runs through the village towards Roebuck and up to Will's Neck.

Stogumber was famous for its ale brewed with water from a nearby medicinal spring. Tradition claims that these waters once cured a man of leprosy. On a rather grimmer note, local folk believed that Monmouth and his men once took part in a battle here so fierce that the field ran red with blood and that some of Monmouth's unfortunate followers were hanged from nearby Heddon Oak — one of those local stories handed down to successive generations acquiring increasingly lurid details as the years go by. At Christmastide the villagers here and around looked forward to the lively and entertaining visits of the Crowcombe Mummers (*see* Crowcombe).

Stogursey

This small village lying between the Quantocks and the sea in gently rolling countryside was formerly a thriving town. As it declined the old shops were adapted for use as private residences. 'Stogursey' is a corruption by mellow, Somerset tongues of Stoke Courcy, a name derived from the landowning de Courcy family. A member of this family, John de Courcy, sailed from England to conquer Ulster during the reign of Henry II.

In Saxon times the manor of Stogursey was held by a thane named Brixi, but after the Norman Conquest it was given to William de Falaise. A small priory was founded which probably had a prior and 2 or 3 monks and functioned as a cell of a Benedictine Abbey in Normandy. By 1324 it consisted of a hall, prior's chamber, store room, kitchen, bakery, brewery and barn. After a later period under

Crown control it was made over to Eton College in 1440, and the College still retains the land and appoints clergy to the living. Today the priory has almost vanished, but the monks' round dovecot remains.

Stogursey Castle, surrounded by a moat supplied by a stream which once turned the wheel of Castle Mill, is now a romantic ruin. The parish church of St Andrew is impressive in its size and style, possessing remarkable Norman arches and great architectural variety. Among other interesting features are its magnificent west window, ancient effigies and a sanctuary ring for the refuge of wrong-doers.

In the 12th century a bad Norman baron named Fulke de Breauté organised a band of robbers who went around the countryside terrorising innocent folk, but Hubert de Burgh put an end to these antics. After the Monmouth Rebellion two men of Stogursey were publicly executed and there are records of the grisly instructions outlined in minute detail for those who had to perform the task.

The almshouses were founded by Sir William Poulett and rebuilt in the 19th century. Suspended above the almshouses is the Ding-Dong Darling bell which sounded daily at 6.00 a.m. and 6.00 p.m. for 500 years. A bell rope dangled in the bellringer's bedroom, presumably allowing him to perform his duties from the convenience of a nice, warm bed. It is rumoured that this bell, in common with a number of others around the county, had a will of its own, refusing to 'ding' if the portents were wrong.

The story goes that the Devil rides the hills around Stogursey. Far back in the mists of time the frightened inhabitants of Nether Stowey sought refuge in Stogursey Castle from a plague of hungry giants who lived beneath a mound. Feeling a trifle peckish after the villagers had left for the safety of Stogursey Castle, the giants emerged from their hiding place to rout them out. Reducing the solid castle to ruins was no trouble at all for these ogres, who scooped up their hapless victims by the handful, then turned and strolled home happily munching.

Rather more benign is Wick Barrow, 2 miles to the north of the village which is colloquially known as Pixies' Mound, a gathering place for the Little People. It is said that a passing labourer once heard the plaintive sound of weeping, and his eye fell upon a miniature spade which had broken. After mending it he returned it to the self same spot for its owner to find. Next day a freshly baked cake was waiting for him as a reward for his kindness.

Stoke Pero

The tiny Exmoor settlement of Stoke Pero, in will o' the wisp country to the south of Porlock, has long captured the romantic imagination on account of its remoteness. At about 1,013 feet above sea level, the quaint little church has won the reputation of being the loneliest and highest on Exmoor. It is recorded that timber for the barrel beamed roof was transported from Porlock by a hardworking donkey called Zulu. The church was rebuilt in 1897 and further renovated in 1958.

The place derives its name from 'Stoc', indicating an enclosure or settlement, and 'Pero' from the Pyrhou, Pyro, Piro or Perow family to whom the land was granted at the time of the Conquest.

Stoke St Gregory

Stoke St Gregory stands above Sedgemoor Old Rhyne 2½ miles north east of North Curry and was formerly known as East Curry. Whereas North Curry had its annual custom of a Reeve's Feast whereby everyone present was invited to eat and drink as much as they chose to the burning of a candle, this village had its Stoke Club Pudding, an oven baked plum pudding, associated with the festivities of Stoke St Gregory Club Day.

Its church of St Gregory is similar to that of North Curry, built during the Middle Ages. The arcades and arches of the central octagonal tower are considered very good, while outside the tower are figures of the Apostles set in niches in 1888. It has interesting bench ends and a Jacobean pulpit depicting Time, Faith, Hope, Charity and the Virgin and Child.

Slough Farm, to the north, was a small Tudor manor house constructed of bonded lias and Ham Hill stone. It has a two storey gabled porch and windows with mullions.

Stoke St Mary, *see* **Orchard Portman**

Stoke-sub-Hamdon

Stoke-sub-Hamdon, situated in a fork between the A303 and the A3088, really comprises East Stoke and West Stoke. This lovely two-part village lies beneath Hamdon Hill, which provided the pleasing honey coloured stone used in the construction of some of east Somerset's finest buildings (*see* Norton-sub-Hamdon). This stylish village is constructed of Ham Hill stone and has some delightful 17th century houses with mullioned windows and well proportioned gables. The beautiful church of St Mary is one of the most ancient and interesting in the county and contains good examples of wide ranging periods of church architecture.

There was a fives court behind the Fleur-de-Lis inn, constructed when the playing of fives against church walls was discouraged. John Pakmer and Fredric Fane, who were the village champions, claimed to be the champion fives players for England in 1855.

Stoke-sub-Hamdon Priory was constructed of the famous local stone in the 14th and 15th centuries. It formerly housed the priests of the chantry of St Nicholas in nearby Beauchamp, a manor house no longer in existence. The Priory is now in the care of the National Trust.

Stolford

The tiny village of Stolford lies on the coast to the west of the Parrett estuary in a wild and spacious area full of interest and character. There is a tremendous tide range with the water retreating 3 or 4 miles to surge back over the flats very swiftly. The attraction of this coastline is its breezy, open aspect and the special nature of the light which catches reflections in the vast mudpools exposed at low tide. The area enjoys some spectacular sunsets.

Because of these wide expanses of oozing mud, the fishermen of Stolford evolved a special 'Mud Horse' which enabled them to get across the difficult surfaces to reach their nets. The fishermen leant on these upright sledge-like structures and pushed them forward to make their way across the muddy foreshore.

Around 2,500 B.C. the coastline off Stolford was covered in forest and at low tide traces of this submarine forest can still be detected. Nearby Stert Island is now a National Nature Reserve for wildfowl.

New roads lead across to Hinkley Point atomic power station, which gives the illusion of rising abruptly from the sea bed.

Stolford, mud horse

Stoughton, *see* **Wedmore**

Stratton-on-the-Fosse

Stratton-on-the Fosse lies directly on the straight course of the Roman Fosse Way between Radstock and Shepton Mallet. Its church, dedicated to St Vigor, is one of just two in Britain to honour the 6th century Bishop of Bayeux in this way. The 17th century Stratton House was formerly a possession of the Long family of Wiltshire. However, the main attraction of the area is the magnificent Downside Abbey. The Benedictines originated in Douai in 1607, came to England in 1795 and acquired the Downside estate in 1814. New buildings were added as the community and the famous public school grew.

When coal was being mined hereabouts, rather short lived canal systems were planned and built. However, dug out sections of the Dorset and Somerset Canal between here and Frome were never fully linked, and the scheme was aborted.

Sutton Bingham, *see* **East Coker**

Sutton Montis, *see* **South Cadbury**

Tainfield, *see* **Kingston St Mary**

Tarr Steps, *see* **Hawkridge and Winsford**

Tatworth

This little village to the south of Chard, close to Somerset's borders with Dorset and Devon, traditionally held candlelight auctions on Old Lady Day (April 6th). The Stowell Court gathered at the Pop Inn where an inch of candle was lit and auctioning took place until the flame went out. The last bidder obtained the land for a year at the price he offered. Any attempts to interfere with the progress of the candle by coughing, breathing deeply or causing a draught in some way were severely frowned upon and would probably merit a fine.

The story is told of a villager who had fallen on hard times, who desperately wanted to rent the fine watercress beds at No Man's Land. His friends, who wanted to help him pull off this coup made unsuccessful attempts to influence the flame, but received stern warnings. In final desperation the poor farmer threw back his head in readiness for an enormous sneeze, whereupon he was sent to the doorway to sneeze politely into his handkerchief. This excited his dog which wagged its tail and barked, causing the candle to flicker and die at just the right moment. No one could accuse a poor, dumb animal of cheating, and his owner won the deal.

Tellisford, *see* **Farleigh Hungerford**

Templecombe, *see* **Milborne Port**

Tintinhull

This picturesque, but now expanding village 5 miles to the north west of Yeovil has some delightful old houses, some of which are situated around a triangular village green. Its beautiful 13th century church of St Margaret's incorporates a variety of styles and has a massive tower on the north side.

Tintinhull Court, the medieval rectory, was extensively rebuilt in the 17th century when it was given a stone facade, and mullioned, transomed windows surmounted by hood moulds were added. The Dower House was constructed in the symmetrical, classical style by the Napper family, who had risen to join the ranks of the gentry. Along Farm Street is Tintinhull House, an old farmhouse dating from 1630, which was converted by the Nappers in the early 18th century. Considered to be one of the most pleasing and perfect examples of its kind, it is now in the care of the National Trust. Its attractive formal gardens were laid out in the 20th century.

Tivington, *see* Selworthy

Tolland

Just to the west of Lydeard St Lawrence is the pretty little village of Tolland with a stream rising in the Brendons flowing through the middle. Its little 13th century church, much restored in the 19th century has an old font, some medieval tiles and a sundial.

There is a romantic tradition that James Turberville, Bishop of Exeter, was banished to Gaulden Manor (or Goldern Manor) in the 16th century on account of refusing to take the Oath of Supremacy to Queen Elizabeth. In fact the house was built in the 17th century by John Turberville, a lawyer from London. In 1647 it housed a detachment of Parliamentary troops. John Turberville placed on record that 'a barrel of good beare trembles at the sight of them,' and that the place had degenerated into 'nothing but a rendezvous of tobacco and spittinge'. The place is now known as Gaulden Farm.

Treborough, *see* Roadwater

Trull, *see* Bradford-on-Tone

Uphill, *see* Brean and Cossington

Upton

The village of Upton lies in picturesque surroundings in the lovely Haddeo Valley, about 5 miles to the north east of Dulverton. Work started on the construction of the Wimbleball Reservoir in 1974 and it was completed in 1979, at the cost of £11 million. With a capacity of 892 million gallons of water, and stocked with trout, Wimbleball Lake has now mellowed into the landscape and has become an amenity area with boating and fishing. There are superb views from the top of Haddon Hill.

Only the ivy clad west tower and base of the nave and chancel remain of the old church of St James, for the church was removed to Rainsbury.

Upton, Wimbleball Reservoir

Upton Noble

Situated to the north east of Bruton between the A359 and the main Taunton railway line, the village of Upton Noble commands fine views towards Alfred's Tower, close to the Somerset/Wiltshire border.

At the eastern end of the village is a five bay house with cross windows dating from about 1700. At the opposite end of the village a house of 1711 has mullioned windows and a pedimented doorway.

The church of St Mary Magdalene has a tower south of the nave with a saddleback roof.

Wadeford, *see* Whitestaunton

Wambrook

Formerly in Dorset, Wambrook, about 2 miles to the west of Chard, is in an area of steep terrain on a north to south ridge, and is approached by narrow, winding lanes. The place was known as Awambruth in 802, with Lower Wambrook becoming known as Haselcombe in the late 12th century.

Christopher Marraker, rector of Wambrook (1591-1621) was tutor to Sir Simonds D'Ewes, the antiquarian writer born at nearby Chardstock. Although a man of learning, he was criticised by parishioners as having 'no regard for the souls of his scholars'. Perhaps the Wambrook folk were too critical, or perhaps they did not have much luck with their rectors, for John Marraker (1555-91) was incapable of speaking up clearly and made free with one of his female parishioners; Gamaliel Chase (1621-45) was thrown into prison first by the Parliamentarians and then by the Royalists; while William Randall was described as 'an idle, sottish fellow'.

The little church of St Mary has a rounded, arched doorway, 13th century font, a blocked up north window with Somerset tracery and some old bench ends. A mile to the north of the village is Weston Farm dating from Tudor times.

Wambrook Farm at Higher Wambrook has handsome stone buildings with high gables, including an unusual granary. The old sluices are still in existence here.

Washford, *see* Old Cleeve

Wayford

Close to the Dorset border, commanding fine views across the beautiful Valley of the Axe and Pilsdon Pen, the tiny village of Wayford straggles along a hillside lane which now peters out into a track offering a pleasant walk past Ashcombe Farm to neighbouring Winsham. The Manor Dairy Farm and a cottage to the east of the church are thought to be early 17th century, while most of the other houses date from the 19th century. The former parsonage house, described in 1606 as being a mansion with a barn, garden and orchard, was dismissed by an early 19th century rector as being 'too small for my large family'. The 13th century church of St Michael at the centre of the village is a plain, stone building, mostly rendered. The chancel had to be rebuilt after falling down in 1846.

Wayford Manor, with its medieval court and well, may once have been a Priests' House and contains various features reminiscent of Montacute. The gardens and Wayford Rhododendron Woods, which have magnificent specimens of trees and shrubs, are a delight to visitors.

The physician and notable eye specialist Dr Daubeney Turberville (1612-96), was born at Wayford and occupied the manor house. His patients included such illustrious people as Samuel Pepys and Princess Anne. On his death he left £100 for the purchase of land to provide funds for the poor, which were distributed on Christmas Day. The charity later became known as Turberville's Educational Foundation.

Wedmore

The village of Wedmore stands on a long, low fertile 'island' above the moors between the Mendips and Poldens. In earlier times when the sea extended as far as Glastonbury this really was an island with water lapping around its shores. When the sea retreated, the waterways eroded away the softer rocks, leaving projections of harder rocks such as this dotted across the Somerset plain.

With its close proximity to the Mark Causeway, Wedmore enjoyed early importance. Its geographical advantages were recognised and it was an obvious site for King Alfred to build his palace. Wedmore achieved a permanent niche in our country's history in 878 when the treaty was signed between Alfred and the

Danes; the Danish leader Guthrum was baptised and underwent the chrisom-loosing ceremony transforming him from a pagan warmonger to a Christian leader of his settled people. This victory was commemorated in Wedmore's church in more recent times with the words:

> 'Alfred the King at Wedmore made Peace
> Death of Alfred 901. Edward Seventh 1901.'

As the natural centre of the Isle, Wedmore was once a manorial borough. A Court Leet was held annually here with portreeves, ale tasters, bread weighers and a hayward being appointed. This ceremony continued until 1913. Echoes of the past survive today in the pleasing central area known as The Borough. This village, with its fine stone houses, high walls and attractive lanes has been widely by-passed by modern highways; an advantage which has given the place a rare distinction all of its own. It is surprising, perhaps to learn that the religious reformer Hannah More, who established a Sunday School here in 1799 experienced much aggravation and described the place as 'depraved and shocking'.

It is known that a church existed here before the end of the 11th century. The ancient church constructed in the shape of a cross has a sturdy tower, a Jacobean pulpit and a particularly fine south doorway. The mural of St Christopher which seems to be one painting covered by another depicts the religious message to the background of a maritime theme with mermaids, fish and ships, A 10th and 11th century hoard of coins was discovered in the churchyard.

Wedmore possesses two beautiful old crosses. One stands in the churchyard; the other, which has a canopied head, is situated outside the house where Judge Jeffreys is thought to have lodged. There is a third cross at Stoughton, a mile to the north.

The village has houses attractively situated around an open green. The 17th century Porch House has casement windows and an imposing Georgian porch. This was where the surgeon John Westover lived, and adjoining his house is the residence built to accommodate and treat mental patients; a rare and caring enterprise which worked extremely well.

Mudgeley Hill, about 1½ miles to the south of the village, offers a vantage point from which to savour this distinctive and agreeable moorland scene.

To the west of Wedmore lies the village of Mark, with its fine 13th century church and splendid tower soaring impressively above the village and surrounding countryside.

West Buckland

West Buckland, to the east of Wellington, was one of the villages to possess a Holy Thorn Tree, originally taken as a cutting from the Glastonbury Thorn (*see* Whitestaunton), which was said to have sprouted from the staff of Joseph of Arimathea. The village, formerly named 'Bocland' knew importance in Saxon times as 'lands in possession of the King'.

The West Buckland Hoard, containing a bronze bracelet, torque, palstave and scabbard, was accidentally discovered about a century ago in the course of excavating a drain. Around the same time, an unfortunate blind woman of the village was reckoned to be responsible for all ills around the neighbourhood, until a farmer whose cows were in decline was instrumental in having her removed to the Wellington workhouse.

Today this formerly remote village finds itself close to the busy M5, near an intersection.

West Camel, *see* Queen Camel

West Coker

West Coker straddles the A30 between Yeovil and Crewkerne and has a spacious church with a medieval tower and horn windows used when glass was rare and expensive. There is a Jacobean pulpit and bench ends dating from 1633.

The beautiful Ham Hill stone manor house in Manor Street was built in 1457 when its predecessor burnt down. Various alterations and additions were made in 1591, 1600, 1875 and 1910. This manor house, which belonged to the Earls of Devon, was burnt down and pillaged in 1457 as a result of a dispute with villagers, who were stirred into action by the rector. The estate was acquired around 1600 by John Portman. There are some beautiful buildings around the village which had connections with the manor. Manor Farm's barn, dating from 1764 has unusual medieval windows thought to have been used originally in some nearby monastic building. The motel occupies the site of the original old rectory (not to be confused with the new 'Old Rectory') which was built over a medieval dwelling with cellars.

West Coker, like East Coker was a great centre of flax and hemp production and sailcloth weaving was a cottage industry. 'Coker' sailcloth became famous all over the world.

In common with some neighbouring villages, the modern houses being built these days blend in well with traditional styles of architecture and building materials.

Just to the north east of the village is the site of a Roman villa, close to a Roman road, and on the site of an Iron Age encampment. Nearby North Coker has some picturesque cottages and a fine old mill.

West Huntspill, *see* Huntspill

West Luccombe, *see* Luccombe

Westonzoyland

Westonzoyland, situated in a landscape of rhines and pollarded willows to the south of the Poldens, was a part of Glastonbury manor, known as 'Sowy' in earlier times. 'Sow', 'Sowe' or 'Zoy' incorporated in local names was derived from the name of a stream which has now gone. The monks of Glastonbury encouraged the tenants to co-operate in intensive land reclamation schemes in the 12th and 13th centuries which created rich watermeadows providing new pastureland and fertile areas for hay and corn production.

This is the closest village to the site of Monmouth's defeat at the fierce and bloody Battle of Sedgemoor in 1685. James, Duke of Monmouth, the illegitimate and charismatic son of Charles II, planned a stealthy advance and surprise attack on the Royalist camp in the early hours of the morning of July 6th. However, the plan went awry when the local guides failed to find the way across the final and crucial stretch of water known as the Bussex Rhine. The Royalist camp was alerted, pandemonium broke out and the Rebels found themselves in a weak position on the wrong side of the water. They were defeated during the battle which ensued and their leaders fled from the battlefield. Mythology has it that Monmouth had been warned by a fortune teller to 'beware the Rhine', but that he felt comfortably distanced from that river in England's West Country. Be that as it may, these harrowing events were followed by a cruel period of retribution, with the notorious Judge Jeffreys meting out his distinctive brand of rough justice, with most of his victims being hanged, drawn and quartered and their earthly remains subjected to further humiliations. Local folk were caught up in these events whether they liked it or not. Immediately after the battle five hundred wounded and dying men were carted to the church and locked inside. 'After ye prissoners was gon out' they were instructed to fumigate the place with frankincense, saltpetre and resin. Villagers were paid to ring out the bells of thanksgiving for a Royalist victory and for Monmouth's capture.

Not surprisingly, the place is steeped in Sedgemoor ghost stories, mostly related to fugitives fleeing from the bloody battlefield, travelling in an easterly direction, wearing cavalier type hats and boots with cloaks a-flying. Monmouth's own ghost is seen either as a galloping horseman in full flight, with his features plainly discernible or as a headless figure stumbling along on foot. It is claimed that eerie, ghostly voices have been heard echoing across the area of the old Bussex Rhine, rallying the Rebels to come and fight.

There are modern memorials to these tragic happenings and there have been a number of re-enactments of the battles, notably in 1985 as part of the 'Pitchfork Rebellion' festivities. In retracing these events it is important to remember that the landscape has been altered considerably since that time. The original channel known as the Bussex Rhine has long since been filled in, and the present watercourse bearing that name was not in existence at the time of the battle.

Surely no church in Britain can have a more poignant link with our country's history than this one. The church, built by Abbot Bere of Glastonbury, has a 100 foot tower rising dramatically to dominate the village and the landscape for miles around. With its medieval roof, its screen, complete with loft and rood, it is reckoned to be one of the finest churches in the county.

Westonzoyland's old Upping Stone used for the convenience of the Devil when mounting his black stead was reputed to be immovable. They say there is no smoke without fire, but anyone hoping to examine it today will be in for a disappointment — for a Bridgwater man who spotted its potential for the manufacturing of chimneypieces removed it — without any difficulty.

Today this village of the Sowy Island in the Somerset Levels is a blend of ancient and modern, a focal point for those who come to see for themselves the spot that played a decisive role in tipping the scales of our country's destiny.

Westonzoyland, Sedgemoor Memorial

Westport

The 2½ mile long Westport Canal was completed in 1840, connecting the navigable part of the River Parrett south of Langport to the new canal port of Westport, charmingly situated in meadowland between Curry Rivel and Ilminster. At Westport there was space to turn the barges around, and they loaded and unloaded at wharves where there were cranes and sturdily built warehouses. Goods destined for Ilminster and beyond were then transported by road. Incoming goods included coal, culm, slate, salt, food, machinery, bricks and building equipment, while outgoing cargoes included flax, wheat, cider, wool, willows, elm wood and building stone.

Rope and twine from Bridport bound for the American continent was brought overland to this inland port to be taken by barge to Bridgwater. It went up the coast to Bristol, then through the canal system to the Mersey before being loaded onto ocean going ships in Liverpool. In former times the inn at Westport would have been busy with boatmen and wharf handlers who lived in nearby cottages (*see* Barrington).

Stern competition from the railway, which arrived hereabouts in 1853, together with problems created by drainage schemes, hastened the decline of the canal and it closed in 1880. Today the port buildings serve other uses and beautifully constructed bridges carry roads over the choked-up wide canal bed.

West Quantoxhead

Lying at the seaward head of the Quantocks, West Quantoxhead is also known as St Audries, a name derived from St Etheldreda, to whom the church was dedicated. She was also a saint who somewhat incongruously lent her name to the uncomplimentary word 'tawdry', which originally described the cheap lace on sale at St Audrey's fair.

The village virtually disappeared in the 19th century when the manor of St Audries was bought Sir Peregrine Acland. The Tudor style Victorian mansion, completed in 1872 and set in pleasing, well wooded parkland sloping towards the sea, is now in use as a girls' school. John Norton designed the mansion and the church which replaced a delapidated building. A former rector, the Rev J.R. Vernon, who was also the author of *The Harvest Of A Quiet Eye*, is buried in the churchyard.

A little stream sparkles through meadowland and leafiness to tumble over the cliff and join the sea. Just off-shore is a submerged forest with trunks still visible. Today the area is enjoyed by holidaymakers and campers who use the facilities provided here, close to the beach.

Whitelackington, *see* Seavington St Mary

Whitestaunton

Narrow, winding lanes bright with wayside flowers lead the way to the unspoilt and peaceful village of Whitestaunton, situated at the eastern end of the Blackdown Hills, with its 15th century church, old manor house and lake in a woodland setting, now colonised by rooks. In springtime the air is alive with birdsong.

It is hardly surprising that beautiful legends of Biblical significance grew up round the place. Joseph of Arimathea is said to have thrust his staff into the ground at Glastonbury, and the staff reputed to have been grown from one of the spray of thorns from Christ's crown, took root and subsequently bore the 'holy thorn' said to burst into bloom on Christmas Eve. Cuttings were taken and distributed all around Somerset. The Whitestaunton tree flourished and attracted pilgrimage. Similarly, the waters of St Agnes Well are said to possess healing qualities and it was once customary for bread to be distributed to the poor beside the well.

During the reign of Charles I, the vicar, Joseph Greenfield, was seized and imprisoned at Ilminster for supporting the king. His son, the vicar of neighbouring Combe St Nicholas, having been told that his father would be released on payment of a ransom duly delivered the money and was promptly thrown behind bars with his father.

The attractions of this delightful corner of Somerset were appreciated by the Romans who built a number of villas around the area, including one here. Evidence of even earlier occupation is Whitestaunton Camp, an earthworks out on the Chard to Yarcombe road. Part of another Roman villa was discovered at nearby Wadeford, a scattered village to the east, which is thought to have derived its name from the locally grown woad plant, used in dyeing cloth.

Wick Barrow, *see* **Stogursey**

Will's Neck, *see* **Aisholt and Upton**

Wimbleball Reservoir, *see* **Brompton Regis and Upton**

Wimblestone, *see* **Shipham**

Winsford

Winsford, with its packhorse bridges, charming thatched cottages, impressive church and lovely old Royal Oak Inn, set in wild moorland between Exford and Exton is considered by many to be the prettiest of Exmoor's villages. Situated at the convergence of the River Exe and the Winn Brook, it derives its name from the ford of the Winn. A house opposite the Wesleyan Chapel bears a plaque informing us that the Socialist politician Ernest Bevin was born here.

Six routes lead to the village, which knew prosperity in the early 17th century. Around these parts it was wise to wear sprays of oak leaves on Oak Apple Day (May 29th), to avoid being pinched, punched or pushed into the stinging nettles. It was a special day when the bridles of horses would be garlanded with oak apples and children festively dressed would turn up at school to chant the customary demand:

'It's the 29th of May,
It's Oak Apple Day,
If you don't give us a holiday
We'll all run away!'

before being given the day off.

Another fruitful custom was observed at Allerntide, in October, when children, sometimes with faces blackened, would go around the cottages begging for 'Allern apples'.

The wild and windy Winsford Hill to the south west of the village offers an impressive vantage point from which to savour the unspoilt, wild moorland. In a National Trust section of landscape is a Bronze Age group of barrows known as the Wambarrows and the Caractacus Stone. Dating from the 5th or 6th century, the stone bears the inscription 'Carataci nepus' meaning 'a descendant of Caractus'. This is taken to be British chieftain who defied the Romans, although some historians point out that Caractacus or Caradoc was a common Celtic name.

From the village a lane leads 3 miles southwards to Tarr Steps, a stone clapper bridge across the River Barle. This beautiful bridge, which some people think to be the oldest in England, has seventeen spans and is 180 feet long. An old guidebook stated, 'He who would see old Exmoor must visit Tarr Steps'. These days thousands of visitors carry out this piece of advice.

Winsford, the Royal Oak

Winsham

The pleasant village of Winsham is situated in the Axe Valley to the south east of Chard and is thought to date back to Saxon times. Originally a small, thriving town, its long main street leads up to the old market cross which has always been the hub of village life, and where five lanes converge. The church, situated half way down this long street, consists of a nave and chancel with a central tower. The road continues southwards down the hill and across a little stone bridge over the gentle River Axe, which also denotes the boundary between Somerset and Dorset. Quite a number of Winsham's original houses suffered fire damage and have been rebuilt at various times. Today it emerges as a very friendly place with pleasing stone and thatched cottages.

In former times Winsham benefitted from being close to Forde Abbey, just over the Dorset border, and it was also an important centre for the manufacturing of West of England cloth. Its decline towards the end of the last century was brought about by the rise of the cloth industry in the industrially developing north and the final blow came when Winsham was bypassed by the railway, the London and South Western Railway having refused to build a station there.

Winsham, which formerly had three inns now has just one, The Bell, and the other buildings have been adapted for use as private residences. Once a variety of shops catered for the needs of villagers and boots, baskets and harnesses were made. There was someone to sweep your chimney, cut your hair, assist you into the world and attend to you on the way out. Today there is just a post office-cum-general stores and villagers look to Chard and other nearby towns to cater for wider needs.

Older villagers talk of the good old days when the streets were bustling on a Saturday night and the pubs were crowded with cheery young folk from the outlying farms and hamlets to attend the weekly 'hop'. Things are rather quieter down Winsham way these days, but older villagers still meet informally by the old market cross for a gossip and a joke and enjoy a walk along those leafy, well loved lanes.

Witham Friary

The pleasant little village of Witham Friary lies near the source of the River Frome to the south west of the town of Frome, and from here there are pleasing views across the vale to Penselwood and Alfred's Tower.

Situated in Selwood Forest, it was chosen as the site of the first Carthusian monastery to be founded in England. Its foundation around 1178 was Henry II's act of atonement to the church for the murder of Thomas à Becket. The Carthusians were a most austere and devoted group of monks living humbly and in great simplicity. Their third and most notable prior, Hugh of Avalon, was here for 6 years before becoming Bishop of Lincoln, and he was canonised as St Hugh of Lincoln. He loved Witham and returned here for periods of retreat. One of the monks serving under St Hugh was Brother Eynard, who lived to the remarkable age of 125 years. In 1283 Witham Friary was given a permit to work the lead mines around Charterhouse in the Mendips. When it was dissolved in 1539 it passed into the possession of the Hopton family.

Today only the church and the dovecote to the south of the church are left to remind us of the site of England's first Charterhouse.

Withiel Florey

To the south of Luxborough, and in an area once exploited for its iron ore, is the tiny hamlet of Withiel Florey where the miners once lodged. Approached by very steep, narrow lanes and amidst spectacular scenery, this is the real heart of the Brendons with its own particular charm. The Norman church of St Mary has a 13th century tower.

Withycombe

Approached through steep, deep set lanes with high hedges, the picturesque village of Withycombe is situated to the south of Carhampton on the lower slopes of the Brendons. Streams rising in the vicinity of Black Hill and Rodhuish Common pass through the village with its attractive colour-washed cottages and neat little church to join the River Pill and emerge in Blue Anchor Bay, just to the east of Blue Anchor.

The mainly 13th century church has a low, massive tower, a Norman font and a beautiful carved screen. Sandhill Manor House, dating from around 1588 and now known as Sandhill Farm, was formerly the seat of the Escott family. It was also the one-time home of Joan Carne, suspected of being a witch and reputed to have murdered her three husbands. The story goes that after her death in 1612 the mourners returned here to find her ghost busy in the kitchen. Although her spirit was 'laid' in a nearby pond she is said to return to her old home each year. There is a brass to her in the church of St Nicholas.

Withypool

There is a wry old saying to the effect that the Exmoor village of Withypool enjoys four harvests — 'snow, frost, rain and muck!' Described by a guidebook of 1907 as 'one of the lonely outposts of civilisation on Exmoor', it lies charmingly set in a wooded hollow about 4 miles to the south of Exford. Its name denoted its situation on the banks of the River Barle; 'a willow fringed pool'.

Windswept Withypool, with its pretty miscellany of cottages, church and pleasing bridge across the river, contrasting with its superb, wild setting is much appreciated by those who like unspoilt places, and is a favourite haunt of anglers.

Before the time of the Norman Conquest, Exmoor was a game reserve and Withypool functioned as a moorland capital until the latter part of the 17th century, with the village inn serving as an administrative meeting place. At the time of Domesday, Dodo, Almer and Godric were recorded as being the three 'foresters of Widepolla', and farming, forestry and quarrying evolved as the main industries of the area.

This small, hilly village, steeped in the spirit of Exmoor, was the home of Walter Raymond, one of Somerset's favourite writers who was born in Yeovil in 1852. From his cottage here he wrote of the crafts and characters that he knew and loved so well.

In days of yore Withypool's resident witch was blamed for anything that went wrong — from crop failure to halting wagons. The poor old crone who crept about or spun around like a whirligig lived with her equally strange husband who kept a pet gander and never ventured anywhere without this constant companion in tow. To ward off ill luck from this or any other direction, local folk pressed silver sixpences into the palms of new born babies for protection.

Wiveliscombe

The little market town of Wiveliscombe, close to the Devon border in a pleasing setting of hills, valleys and trout streams, straddles the lower slopes of the Brendons and the Vale of Taunton and commands enchanting views across the River Tone to Wellington and its monument on the Blackdown Hills.

An entry (or more correctly non-entry) in Edward Hutton's *Highways & Byways in Somerset* of 1912 states: 'In good hopes I went on to Wiveliscombe; but of Wiveliscombe I have nothing to say; it is not, perhaps, worth a visit . . .' However, *Murray's Hand Book of Wilts, Dorset & Somerset* of 1856 did find something to say: 'This is a market town of some size in a remote situation among swelling hills, on one of which it hangs, with its feet in a valley. It derives its pretty name from the Saxons, who, according to tradition, built it when driven from the Castle Hill by the Danes . . .' Castle Hill, just east of the town has yielded evidence of Roman occupation with numbers of coins being discovered there.

Now tranquil, the place has had a long history. Just to the south east is an ancient earthworks. As a former Crown possession, the manor was granted by Edward the Confessor to the See of Wells, and it remained in their possession until Elizabeth forced Bishop Godwin to hand it over to her favourite, Sir Walter Raleigh. At the time of the Armada, the townsfolk were put through a 'Dad's Army' type of training in their spare time and by all accounts these Somerset lads were somewhat erratic when it came to handling weaponry. The town emerged from the Civil War relatively unscathed, but many local men lost their lives in the Battle of Sedgemoor and 3 of them were hanged in the town during the cruel aftermath of the Monmouth Rebellion.

The handsome, mellow-toned red sandstone church was rebuilt in 1829, to the regret of some local folk who told of the sad knell sounded by the bells and eerie, wailing sounds from within the old church, interpreted as signifying the dismay of the spirits when the decision was made to pull it down. In the churchyard are the remains of a weathered ancient cross and there are traces of the 14th century Bishops' Palace to the south of the church.

The little town with a number of interesting old houses is ideally situated for exploring the Brendons, Exmoor, the Blackdown Hills and the delightful Vale of Taunton.

Wookey

The village of Wookey is separate from Wookey Hole and lies about 2 miles to the west of Wells on the B3139. Its name was derived from the Old English word 'wocig' meaning a trap for animals. The 12th century church was restored in the 19th century and contains much of interest including the 15th century arcade, some 16th century monuments and a modern organ. On 13th May 1906, a terrific thunderstorm suddenly erupted with lightning shattering the stair turret and causing it to crash through the roof. The congregation miraculously escaped injury.

Mellifont Abbey, formerly the Old Rectory, was an early 19th century house. It was constructed in the Gothic style with brick dressings and had battlements and pointed windows. Nearby Court Farm, dating from the early 16th century contains fragments of a 13th century doorway. East Court is an early 18th century red brick building with an imposing doorway.

A mile to the north east towards Wookey Hole is Glencot, constructed in 1895 in the neo-Tudor style with Ham Hill stone dressings, and built for the owners of Wookey Hole Paper Mills.

Wookey was the birthplace of Cyril Arthur Pearson, who founded *The Daily Express* and other journals. After losing his sight later in life he devoted himself to the welfare of the blind.

Wookey Hole

Wookey Hole, situated to the north east of Wookey, consists of mainly 19th century buildings, and is a place of interest and charm associated mainly with paper making and caves. The pure quality of the Mendip water was found to be particularly suitable for paper making and in the late 18th century there were four paper mills on the River Axe around Wookey. Hodgkinson's near the entrance to the caves, thought to date back to 1610 is reputed to be one of the oldest paper mills in the country. St Cuthbert's Mill, once known as Lower Wookey Mill originated around the end of the 18th century.

Wookey Hole has many caverns accessible only to expert cavers. It is well endowed with fantastic stalactites and stalagmites and has a brilliant turquoise river running through it, which widens into a lake. Today the first three chambers are floodlit and open to the public. One of the best known features, and one which readily captures the imagination is the 'Witch of Wookey'. The legend would have us believe that this once beautiful woman, who sold herself to the Devil, was petrified in stone for eternity by a young monk sprinkling holy water on her and her demon companions. Strangely, excavations revealed the skeleton of a woman near a dagger, sacrificial knife and stalagmite resembling a witch's crystal.

The Mendip caves such as Wookey Hole yield their long held archaeological secrets and give us an insight into life in earliest times. In nearby Hyena Den, once inhabited by Stone Age people, remains of animals going back as far as Palaeolithic times have been excavated. Objects of interest can be seen at the museum here and in Wells.

Today the Show Caves, Museum, Fairground collection and many other facilities offer a popular day out for all the family.

Wookey Hole, the Witch's Kitchen

Woolavington, *see* Cossington

Yarlington

Yarlington, west of Wincanton, lies on secondary roads within a triangle created by the A371, A359 and A303, in lovely, rolling green countryside typical of this part of Somerset. The River Cam rises just to the east near Jack White's Gibbet (*see* Bratton Seymour).

The church of St Mary has a 15th century tower and font, but was mostly rebuilt in 1878. Yarlington House, dating from about 1790 and constructed in brick has a handsome front with broadly spaced bays, a doorway with Tuscan columns and Venetian windows. Today its lovely gardens are open to the public under the National Gardens Scheme.

Yeovilton

Just east of the old Roman town of Ilchester and close to the point where the Hornsey Brook and the River Cam join the River Yeo is the once tranquil village of Yeovilton. It was one of a string of Saxon settlements founded along the Yeo on land projecting above the flood level of the time.

Although the area is sparsely populated, the proximity of the Royal Naval Air Station, established here in 1940, leaves little doubt as to the impact of the 20th century on the world in which we live. Yeovilton Fleet Air Arm Museum houses a fine and growing collection of aircraft, particularly those used in the two World Wars and the Concorde 002.

Bibliography

Boger, E., *Myths, Scenes and Worthies of Somerset*
Burton, S.H., *The West Country*, 1972
Burton, S.H., *Exmoor*, 1969
Coysh, A.W., Mason, E.J. & Waite, V., *The Mendips*, 1954
Dunning, R.W., *A History of the County of Somerset* Volume IV, 1978
Dunning, R.W. *Somerset and Avon*, 1980
Dunning, R.W. *A History of Somerset*, 1983
Dyer, James, *The Penguin Guide to Prehistoric England and Wales*, 1981
Eagle, Dorothy, Carnell, Hilary, *The Oxford Literary Guide to the British Isles*, 1977
Farr, Grahame, *Somerset Harbours*, 1954
Fraser, Maxwell, *Somerset*, 1934
Fraser, Maxwell, *Companion Into Somerset*, 1947
Harper, C.G., *The Somerset Coast*, 1909
Havinden, Michael, *The Somerset Landscape*, 1981
Hawkins, Desmond, *Avalon and Sedgemoor*, 1982
Hutchings, Monica, *Inside Somerset*, 1963
Hutton, Edward, *Highways and Byways In Somerset*, 1912
Legg, R., Collier & Perrott, *Ghosts of Devon and Somerset*, 1974
Little, Bryan, *Portrait of Somerset*, 1969
Maxwell, Donald, *Unknown Somerset*, 1927
Martin, Myles, *Somerset Tales*, 1975
Mee, Arthur, *Somerset*
Murray, Stephen, *Yeovil, Sherborne and the West Country*, 1941
Peel, J.H.B., *Portrait of Exmoor*, 1970
Pevsner, Nikolaus, *South and West Somerset*, 1958
Pevsner, Nikolaus, *North Somerset and Bristol*, 1958
Richmond, W.R., *The Story of Somersetshire*
Storer, Bernard, *The Natural History of the Somerset Levels*, 1985
Tongue, R.L., *Somerset Folklore*, 1965
Waite, Vincent, *Portrait of the Quantocks*, 1964
Webber, Ronald, *The Devon and Somerset Blackdowns*, 1976
Whitlock, Ralph, *Somerset*, 1975
Winbolt, S.E., *Somerset*, 1939
Murray's *Hand-Book Wilts, Dorset & Somerset, 1856*